CHILTON'S repair and tune-up
    the Simca; produced by the
Book Department. 1970.
    Illus. (inc. col.), diags.

Philadelphia, Chilton
        & Co.

Chilton's
Repair and Tune-Up Guide

for the

SIMCA

Illustrated

PRODUCED BY THE AUTOMOTIVE BOOK DEPARTMENT

Managing Editor: JOHN MILTON

Technical Editor/Writer: MARVIN L. GASKILL

CHILTON BOOK COMPANY
PHILADELPHIA   NEW YORK   LONDON

DATE 1970	EDITION 1st	SHELVED AT
TITLE NO. 1 740381	COPY NOS. 01	SIMC
ISBN/PART NO. 0 8019 5535 1		

Contents

CHILTON BOOK COMPANY expresses appreciation to these firms for their generous assistance: CHAMPION SPARK-PLUG COMPANY, Toledo, Ohio; GOODYEAR TIRE & RUBBER COMPANY, Akron, Ohio; CHRYSLER MOTORS CORPORATION, (Simca-Rootes Division), Detroit, Michigan.

New Simca Cars

The Simca-Rootes Division of Chrysler introduced seven new Simca models in 1969. Five of the new cars are front-wheel-drive, two- and four-door sedans, and station wagons of the 1204 Series, using both four-speed and semi-automatic transmissions. The Simca 1118 Gran Luxe (GL) and Gran Luxe Super (GLS) four-door sedans replace the Simca 1000.

Front-Wheel Drive 1204

In addition to the front-wheel-drive system with both manual and semi-automatic transmissions, the 1204 features constant-velocity U-joints that transmit power smoothly to the front wheels. Fully adjustable, four-wheel torsion bar suspension with rack-and-pinion steering, together with radial-ply, 13-inch tires, disc brakes and anti-sway bars, further enhance the 1204's handling capabilities.

The 62 horsepower engine is derived from the 1200-S Bertone Coupe performance engine, a water-cooled OHV four-cylinder power plant with a five-main bearing crankshaft—16 percent heavier—and an aluminum head. Top speed is over 85 mph.

SIMCA 1118

The Simca 1118 sedan has mechanical as well as styling improvements. Its engine is more powerful, with more than an 18 percent increase in displacement—from 944 to 1118 cc. Horsepower is increased to 56, and torque peaks lower at 2600 rpm instead of 3700 for smoother performance.

Roadability is improved by several factors. The front suspension has a new design, creating a very flat ride. The rear suspension has double universals, and each wheel permits a stabilizing, negative-camber during all driving conditions. A stabilizer bar is added to the front suspension. These innovations, coupled with new 13-inch wheels, radial-ply tires and rack-and-pinion steering give the 1118 exceptional highway steadiness and maneuverability with no appreciable sacrifice in its 30-plus mpg fuel economy.

Simca Identification

In all correspondence with your dealer, or when ordering spare parts, the type designation, chassis number, and engine number of the Simca should always be given for proper identification.

Type number, body serial number and body paint for the 1204 are identified by plates attached to the fender apron under the hood. The engine serial number is stamped on the side of the block and the

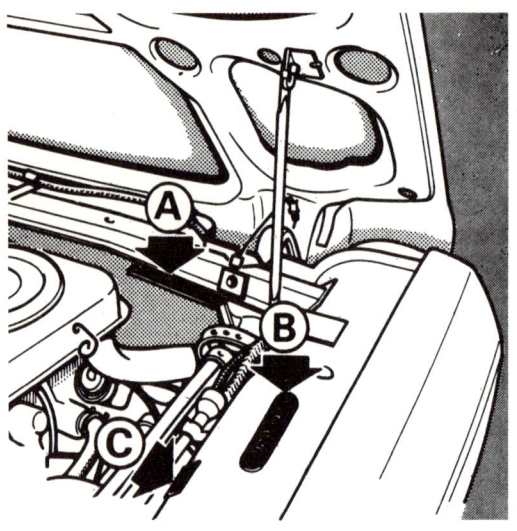

Type serial number (A); body serial number (B).

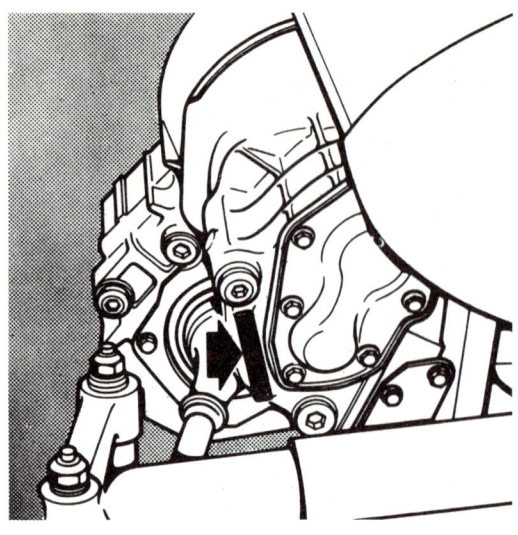

Gearbox serial number.

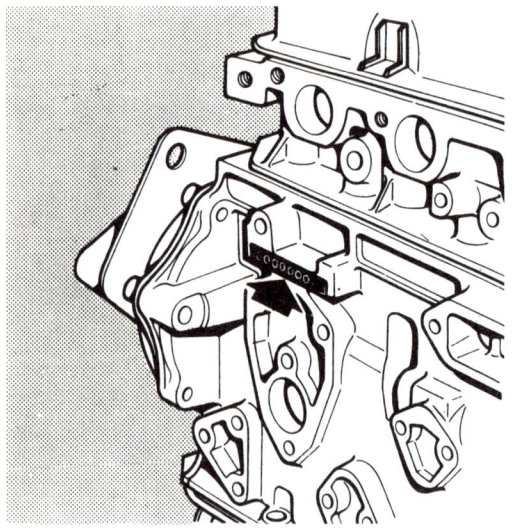

Engine serial number.

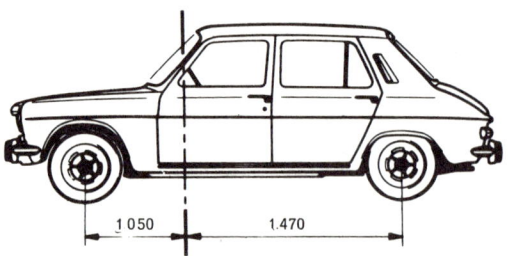

Simca 1204 center of gravity is approximately 42 in. (1.05 mm.) from the front axle, and 57 in. (1.47 mm.) from the rear axle.

General Specifications

Car Model	No. Of Cylinders	Capacity (Cu. In.)	Compression Ratio	BHP	@RPM	Carburetor	Brakes, Front/Rear Disc (DS) Drum (DM)	Electrical System (V)	Track, F/R (In.)	Wheelbase (In.)	Length	Width	Height	Weight (Lbs.)	Tire Size (in.)
1000	4	57.6	7.8:1	52	5400	Solex 32PBIC	DM/DM	12		87.4	155		49	1750	5.60 x 12
1204	4	69	9.6:1	53	5800	Solex 32BISA	DS/DM	12	53/51	99	155	62	58	1984	5.70 x 13
Simca 5	4		8.5:1	65	5200	Solex 32PBIC	DM/DM	12							
1118	4	68.2	9.0:1	56	5600	Solex	DM/DM	12	49/49	87.4	150	58.5	53.4	1795	5.70 x 13

transmission serial number is stamped on the gearbox housing.

Recommended Lubrication

CAUTION: in jacking Simca cars, place jack only at designated re-inforced points behind the front wheels and ahead of the rear wheels. Never jack car on either side at center of body.

Getting continuous top performance from fine machinery requires periodic maintenance using recommended lubricants. Always consult your owner's manual for factory recommended procedures.

Engine oil level is accurately shown on the dipstick only when the engine is warm but not running—preferably after sitting a while to allow oil to drain into sump. Check sump level when re-fueling.

No lubrication fittings are provided on the later model Simca chassis, suspension parts, rack-and-pinion steering, alternator, gearshift control, or electric motors of radiator fan, windshield wipers or heater-defroster, and no lubrication is required for these components.

Simca 1000 ball joints with grease fittings should be lubricated every 12,000 miles.

Replacing the oil filter every 10,000 miles requires care when tightening. One-half turn (by hand only) beyond firm contact should adequately seal the gasket. Check for leaks after starting engine. Using oil of proper viscosity aids cold starting by increasing cranking speed.

Lubricate carburetor linkage at all pivot points with one or two drops of engine oil while moving throttle controls. Oil accelerator pump rods. Disconnect all ball joints, fill cups with high-temperature grease and reconnect. Move linkage back and forth to check for proper functioning.

Lubricate distributor cam with non-corrosive high-temperature grease. Remove distributor cap, lift off rotor and apply a thin coating to the cam. Do not allow grease or dirt to contaminate breaker points.

Maintenance Suggestions

The Appendix presents units of the metric system with the American equiva-lents, matching the precision of each to the nearest 1/100,000. The best preparation for working on any foreign engine is to master the metric system and use a set of metric tools.

Because British terminology for European assemblies and components is most often used, it is best to understand the British wording. If communication with European manufacturers ever becomes necessary, writing the British phraseology will prevent confusion and wrong deliveries. Some terms are given in the text in parentheses, and a more complete listing of British terms and American equivalents is in the Appendix.

Frequent Maintenance Checks

Engine oil:	Check level. Change every 3,000 miles or two months.
Battery fluid:	Check level. Add chemical-free drinking water. Do not over-fill; neutralize spilled acid with baking soda and flush with clean water.
Engine coolant:	Check level. Note presence of sediment. Refill drained radiator with antifreeze solution.
Lubrication:	Hinges and locks, windshield-wiper linkage, carburetor linkage.
Tires:	Check pressure and wear.

6,000-Mile Inspection and Maintenance

General

Leaks:	Visual check for fuel, oil.
Fluid levels:	Transmission, rear axle, master-brake cylinder.
Filters:	Clean fuel pump strainers, sediment bowl, oil-damp air cleaner. Replace air filter cartridge, oil filter.
Lubrication:	Wheel bearings, suspension parts, carburetor linkage, chassis fittings.

Electrical

Battery: Check condition of charge, clean cables.

Ignition

Spark plugs: Inspect, clean or replace, set electrode gap.

Distributor: Lubricate cam, inspect and clean or replace points, reset.

Timing: Check timing and reset if necessary.

Carburetor

Fuel flow: Check for proper jetting and atomization of fuel.

Idle speed: Set idle speed.

Engine

Valve clearance: Check against specifications and reset if necessary.

Crankcase: Inspect crankcase ventilation system.

Fan (or Alternator) belt: Inspect belt and correct the tension if necessary.

Compression: Test for equal compression in all cylinders.

Rocker arm shaft: Check tighteners.

Clutch

Check pedal travel and free play.

Suspension

Control arm ball joints: Check for wear.

Front axle: Check for excessive play.

Wheels

Alignment: Tighten wheel nuts, correct balance, adjust alignment.

Brakes: Test for proper operation, fluid leaks, adequate pedal.

Pads and linings: Remove wheel and inspect. Measure wear.

Tires

Rotate and check pressure.

Battery care. Batteries should be checked periodically for proper output and good connections. A weak power supply lowers the efficiency of the engine and places a greater drag on the generator circuit.

Inspect the battery case for cracks and weakness. A leaky battery should be replaced. With a hydrometer, check the density (specific gravity) of the battery electrolyte. Readings from a fully charged battery will depend on the make but will fall within 1.260 to 1.310. *NOTE: all cells should produce nearly equal readings.* If one or two cell readings are sharply lower, the cells are defective. and if readings continue to be low after charging, the battery must be replaced.

As a battery releases its charge, sulphate ions in the electrolyte become attached to the battery plates, reducing the density of the fluid. The specific gravity of the electrolyte varies not only with the percentage of acid in the liquid, but also with temperature. As temperature increases, the electrolyte expands so that specific gravity decreases. As temperature drops, the electrolyte contracts and gravity increases. To correct readings for temperature variations, add .004 to the hydrometer reading for every 10°F that the electrolyte is above 80° F, and subtract .004 for every 10° F that the electrolyte is below 80°F. The illustration shows the total correction to

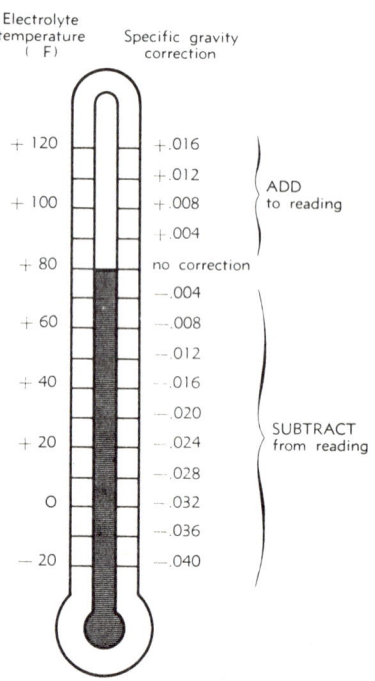

How temperature affects the specific gravity readings of batteries.

make for any temperature above or below 80°F.

The amount of charge remaining in a battery can be roughly determined from the specific gravity ranges shown in the chart below.

Hydrometer readings	Condition
1.260–1.310	Fully charged
1.230–1.250	¾ charged
1.200–1.220	½ charged
1.170–1.190	¼ charged
1.140–1.160	Almost discharged
1.110–1.130	Fully discharged

Perform a light-load voltage test to detect weak cells. First draw off the transient (surface) charge by operating the starter for three seconds and then turning on the low beam lights. After one minute, test each cell (with lights still on) with a voltmeter. A fully charged battery will have no cell voltage below 1.95 volts, and no cell should vary more than .05 volt from the others. A greater variation at full charge indicates a defective cell.

Another battery check involves connecting a charger for three minutes under 40 amperes.

Read the battery voltage with the charger still operating. Voltage over 15.5 v indicates a defective battery. If battery voltage is under this limit and individual cell readings are within 0.1 volt, the battery is usable.

Charging a weak battery is best done by a slow-charge method. If quick charging is attempted, check the cell voltages and the color of the electrolyte a few minutes after charge is started. If cell voltages are not uniform or if electrolyte is discolored with brown sediment, quick charging should be stopped in favor of a slow charge. In either case, do not let electrolyte temperature exceed 120°F.

If high electrical circuit voltage is suspected, the voltage regulator might be cutting in abnormally due to corroded or loose battery connections. The symptoms are hard starting, full ammeter charge, and lights flaring brightly. After cleaning, coat battery terminals with petroleum jelly (vaseline) to prevent recurrence of problem.

Overcharging the battery is a common cause of battery failure. A symptom of overcharging is the frequent need for addition of water to the battery. The generating system should be corrected immediately to prevent internal battery damage.

Cooling system. The engine is water cooled and the cooling system is of the pressure type. A double acting thermostat with an opening temperature of 162°F speeds up engine heating and assumes optimum temperature under all operating conditions.

The radiator of the 1204 is cooled by a four-blade, electrically operated fan. It is powered by a relay, which is actuated by a temperature switch. The switch closes, starting the fan, when the radiator temperature reaches 190.4°F. The switch closes, stopping the fan, when the temperature falls to 174.2°F.

CAUTION: since the fan could start automatically due to radiator temperature rise, even with the engine not running, disconnect the temperature switch for safety while repairs are being made on a warm engine.

Replace radiator coolant once a year, when the entire cooling system should be flushed clean with water. The recommended coolant is a mixture consisting of 40 percent ethylene glycol and 60 percent water. To drain the cooling system, remove the water pump screw. Remove the expansion bottle and empty its contents into the radiator.

When refilling, the heater control must be set at Max heat so that the entire system can be filled. Fill the radiator to the top and put on the cap. Then fill the expansion bottle to the Max mark, no higher. Warm the engine and then check to make sure that the radiator is completely full and the level is between the marks on the expansion bottle.

Effective cooling system protection against rust requires at least a 25 percent solution of the recommended antifreeze (+10°F) through summer and winter. If only water is used, a water pump lubricant and a heavy-duty cooling system protector should be added. Methanol or alcohol alone is not recommended for the cooling system. These agents with their low boiling points evaporate in a short time. Ethylene glycol antifreeze compounds have boiling points close to 400°F, well above the heat range of water-cooled engines. Anti-rust and lubrication additives are helpful in lubricating the water pump and protecting

Capacities and Pressures

Car Model	CRANKCASE		TRANSAXLE		FUEL		Cooling Cap. (Pts.)	TIRE PRESSURES (PSI)		
	Cap. (Pts.)	Oil Press. (Psi)	Cap. (Pts.)	Vis.	Tank Cap. (Gals)	Pump Press. (Psi)		Front	Rear	Spare
1000	5.2	56.9 (@3000 RPM)	3.8	Spirax 90 EP or equivalent	7.9[1]		11.6	16	24	24
1204	4.2				11.09	1.4	6.9	24	26	26
Simca 5	10		2.3		11.4		15	21	23	23
1118	5.3				9.5					

1. 9.5, from body Serial No. J-02247.

metal parts. The rust and foam inhibitors used in antifreeze lose their power with aging, particularly in older engines, with greater rust deposits. Antifreeze, itself, eventually loses its protective properties and becomes an irritant to the cooling system. Replace at the recommended intervals.

Antifreeze is harmful to the oil system. If cooling system fluid has leaked into the engine oil, ethylene-glycol-monobutyl-cellu-solve, available from jobbers, is recommended for flushing the system.

Water condensation in the engine is often caused by limited use of the car. If an engine runs only two or three miles before being shut down, it does not maintain its proper operating temperature long enough to evaporate water that may be present in the crankcase. Regular oil changes will help eliminate water accumulation. Also check the thermostat for too-quick opening. If necessary, change the thermostat for hotter engine operation.

Fan belt adjustment. A tight fan belt will cause rapid wear of the generator and water pump bearings. A loose fan belt will slip and wear excessively, causing noise, engine overheating, and fluctuating generator output. Fan belt tension is correct when light finger pressure deflects the belt one-half inch. An oily or frayed fan belt should be replaced. Remove the belt by loosening the generator mount. Tighten the new belt by properly positioning the generator. Then tighten the mounting. (See Chapter five).

Air cleaner maintenance. Replace paper filter element every 12,000 miles under normal driving conditions and more frequently in severe environments. Do not moisten or oil paper elements. Engines use tons of air even at idle; restriction of air flow inevitably affects engine performance and increases fuel consumption.

Oil-damp type air filters should be washed in solvent, blown dry, and dampened again with oil. Clean every 6,000 miles.

Brake check and adjustment. Check condition of drum brakes by depressing pedal firmly. If pedal travels to within two inches of floor mat and has a hard feel, brake shoes require adjustment or relining. Remove wheel, hub, and drum assembly to check lining. If worn nearly to rivets, reline brakes. If pedal has a spongy feel, the brake system needs bleeding. Check fluid level in master cylinder reservoir, and add fluid if necessary. Adjust drum-type brakes by jacking up the car so the wheels are free to turn. Release the handbrake. Remove the rubber seal. Turn the wheel in a forward direction while turning the notched adjuster cams. When the wheel can barely be turned using one hand, back off the adjuster cams until the wheel turns freely.

Disc brakes do not require adjustment. However, the friction pads in the calipers must be checked for wear every 6,000 miles.

Tighten drum brakes by turning cams in directions shown.

Brake pads should be replaced when one-sixteenth inch, or less, lining remains.

Adjust parking brake when hand lever has a travel greater than ratchet clicks. Fully release hand lever, check cable freedom and loosen equalizer and adjusting nut. Pull lever up three clicks and tighten cable with rear brakes beginning to bind. Check for equal action at both brakes. Lubricate cable.

Wheel and Tire Care

Wheel and Tire Balance

Wheel and tire balance is more critical with respect to tire wear than many drivers realize. Unbalance is the principal cause of tramp, car shake, pounding, and riding roughness. Unbalance often contributes to steering misalignment and damage.

Original balance of the tire and wheel is gradually lost as the tires wear. Severe acceleration, braking, cornering, and side-slipping upset wheel balance in even less time. Wheels also need balancing after tire punctures are repaired.

Check wheel balance each time the tires are rotated—every 6,000 miles—for maximum tire and front end life.

Tire Wear and Storage Notes

Tread design is one of the more important considerations in tire performance. The design affects acceleration, speed, cornering, braking, heat dissipation, wear, noise and related factors. Tread pattern should be checked periodically for premature wear.

Check tread life by placing a penny in a tread groove. If the top of Lincoln's head is completely exposed, the tire should be re-

Excessive wear along tire edges caused by under inflation.

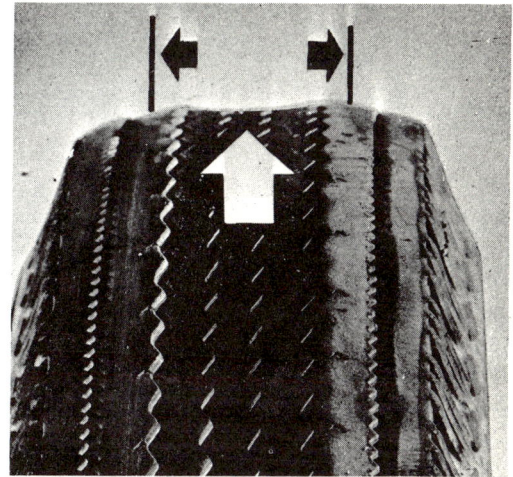

Excessive wear on one side of tire caused by over inflation.

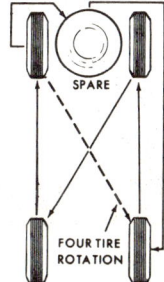

Broken line shows tire rotation without spare.

Tire wear on one side caused by improper camber.

placed or recapped. Ninety percent of tire failure occurs in the last 10 percent of tread life. A more convenient tread wear indicator is the solid crossbars of rubber that show across the tire when the tread pattern has worn to one-sixteenth inch. These bars are now required by federal legislation for all tires.

Storage tips. To avoid shortening service life, tires must be properly stored while they are not in use. These tips will help keep stored tires in good condition.

1. Check the tires for road damage. Remove stones and other objects that may be trapped in the tread grooves. Have any necessary repairs made.

2. Store the tires in a clean, dry, cool, closed, and dark room.

3. Keep the tires away from water, petroleum products such as gasoline and oil, electric motors, and heat sources.

4. Place the tires on their sidewalls on a flat surface. Permanent flat-spotting can result if the tires are stored standing on their treads.

5. Inflation pressure should be reduced to 12 to 16 pounds if tires are to be stored mounted on wheels.

6. White sidewall tires should be placed whitewall to whitewall, one on top of the other, to protect the white rubber from scuffs and dirt.

Abnormal wear across entire tread caused by front end misalignment. If tread is worn in spots, wheel is most likely out of balance.

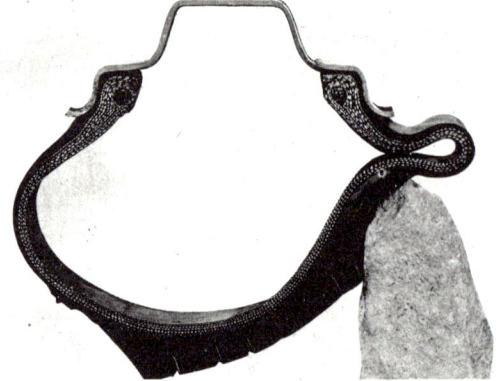

Striking a rock or curb causes bruise damage, particularly to sidewalls.

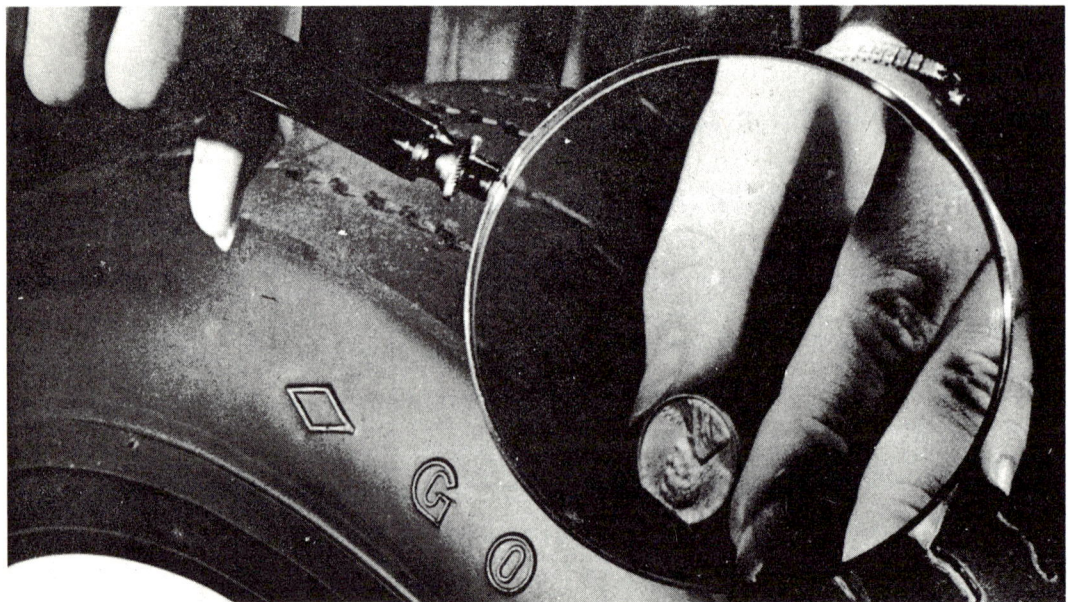

Simple test for tread life. Tires should be replaced if, as shown, coin can hardly be inserted in groove.

Chapter Two

Troubleshooting Checks

Locating No-Start Problems

One frequent cause of the engine not starting is carburetor flooding. To check this, press accelerator to the floor and hold there while starting engine. If the engine starts, the trouble is not caused by carburetor flooding.

When the cause of engine failure is uncertain, the most efficient way to get the engine running again is to follow a series of troubleshooting checks that break no-start problems into four areas—engine cranking, ignition, fuel and compression. Locating the no-start trouble is easily done.

First try to crank the engine with the starter. Slow engine cranking, or none at all, indicates that the trouble is in the battery, cables, switches, or starter. Detailed testing to find the specific defect is provided in the next section of this chapter, TESTING NO-START COMPONENTS.

Engine Cranking System Checks

If engine cranking checked out normal, disconnect a wire from a spark plug, hold it (avoid shock by wearing glove) about one-quarter to one-half inch from the plug terminal, and have the engine cranked over with the ignition switch on. Check for strong, evenly-timed arcs. The ignition system must supply (often through worn parts) an amount of voltage necessary to form a bright spark at the electrode gap. If there is no spark, or if the arc pulse is irregular or weak, the problem is in the ignition system. Special testing for ignition trouble is described in the next section under IGNITION.

With cranking and ignition successfully checked, remove the air cleaner to gain access to the carburetor. Work the throttle linkage up and down. A stream of fuel should spurt from the accelerator jets. If no fuel injects into the carburetor throat after repeated throttle pumping, there is a defect in the fuel system. A less common malfunction is continuous flooding of the carburetor. If the carburetor throat is soaked with gasoline and fumes are heavy, have the motor cranked and check for fuel streaming from the main jet into the intake manifold. This check reveals another type of fuel system trouble. Extensive testing procedures are presented in the next section under FUEL.

The last no-start troubleshooting check is for an infrequent, yet sometimes elusive, problem—no compression. In most cases, compression failures show up in one or two cylinders and are normally not severe enough to prevent starting. However, blow-by into the intake manifold due to a burnt or improperly seated valve can impede the flow of gas vapor into the cylinders and prevent starting. Complete compression failure can be caused by a burnt valve, jumped timing chain, stripped timing gear, a broken camshaft, or possible the improper mating of timing gears in a newly rebuilt engine. Check for compression by removing a spark plug, sealing the piston chamber with a thumb, cork or other object, and crank the engine over. Good compression will gently pop the thumb from the opening. No-compression troubles are analyzed in another section, HARD STARTING, POOR PERFORMANCE—TUNING.

Testing No-Start Components

Once the no-start problem has been located, special testing within that area can directly identify the malfunction while saving expense and valuable time. Each of the units below has a step-by-step troubleshooting test procedure to eliminate the suspicion of working parts and to determine the exact trouble.

Engine Cranking System Checks

The engine-cranking network includes the battery, cables, switches, and starter. The battery and cables are checked first because they are the storehouse and supply of all electrical power, feeding the starter motor, ignition system, lights, and accessories.

Turn on the headlights and crank the engine with the starter. If the lights dim sharply and the cranking slows drastically, either the battery cables are making poor contact or the battery itself is nearly discharged.

If the headlights stay bright but the starter turns slowly or not at all, the starter cables or switches may be faulty or the starter defective. Check the difference in voltage readings taken at the battery and at the starter while the starter is cranking the engine to determine the voltage drop through the cables and solenoid.

Checking cables. Check the connections by carefully working a screwdriver between each cable connector and its terminal post.

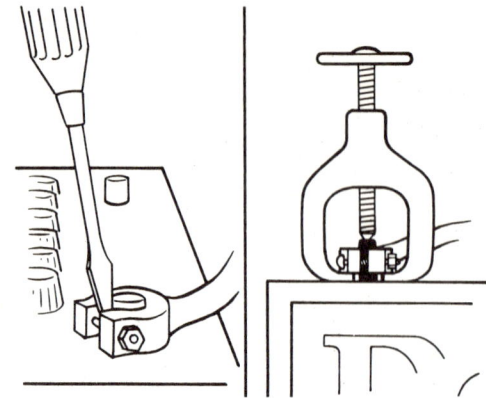

Spreading cable clamp and pulling it from battery terminal.

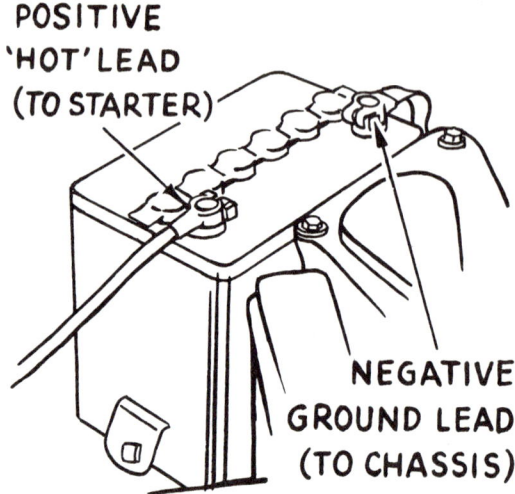

Battery connections.

If the engine cranking improves, the trouble is in the connection.

WARNING: hammering, jarring or prying against the terminal may loosen and short-out the battery plates.

Sometimes an imperfect connection can be identified simply by smoke or vapor rising from corrosion in that area when the starter switch is actuated.

Cleaning cables and terminals should be done with utmost care to prevent damage to the battery. If a cable cannot be removed easily by hand after the clamp bolt is loosened, a small screw-type puller should be used.

Thorough wire brushing or application of a strong baking soda solution will successfully clean terminals and connectors.

CAUTION: cleaning solutions will dam-

age the battery cells if allowed to seep through the vented caps.

Battery test. If engine cranking is unsuccessful after checking out the cable connections, the battery is discharged. A hydrometer reading can quickly tell if any cells are dead. A battery that is normal (though discharged) will have nearly equal specific gravity readings for each cell. (Readings of a fully charged battery range from 1.260 to 1.310, depending on the make.) But if one or two cells have a reading far lower than the others, there is an electrical short circuit within the battery. Tips for charging batteries properly are given in Chapter One under "Battery care."

Once it has been determined that the battery is discharged, the generator and regulator must be checked for proper charging rate as described in Chapter Five, "Electrical Systems."

Checking switches. After the battery and cables have been checked, the starting system switches should be tested.

Test 1. First, bypass the starter switch by running a jump cable or other heavy-gauge lead directly from the hot terminal of the fully charged battery to the input terminal of the solenoid.

DANGER: rings, watches and other metal in contact with the hand can cause severe burns with accidental battery-voltage contact. A heavy, cloth glove offers good protection against burns caused by sudden overheating of the jump cable.

If the starter motor turns when electrical contact is made, the malfunction is in the starter switch or its wiring. If there is no starter response or just a click in the solenoid, make a second test.

Test 2. Cautiously touch the hot cable directly to the starter motor lead. This bypasses the solenoid. In a clutch-type starter assembly, the starter should spin but will not engage the flywheel when the solenoid is omitted from the circuit. If the starter spins, the trouble is in the solenoid unless, in the previous test, the solenoid had clicked. The solenoid serves two simultaneous functions switching power into the starting motor and engaging the starter-clutch assembly. If the solenoid clicked in the first test and the starting motor spun free in the second test, the solenoid is good, and the trouble is a locked or frozen engine. (If starter gear is jammed against the flywheel, place gearshift lever in high gear and gently rock car back and forth.) Getting no response with the hot lead on the starter terminal indicates that the problem is in the starting motor itself.

Starter check. The intensity of the spark at the contact of the hot cable with the starter terminal may help to determine the fault in the motor. A bright, nearly welding flash indicates that there is a shorted circuit within the starting motor. A weak spark, or none at all, points to a poor connection of the motor brushes with the commutator. The brushes could be completely worn. The brush springs could be broken. The commutator could have burnt spots or be dirty or oily.

Chapter Five provides detailed overhaul

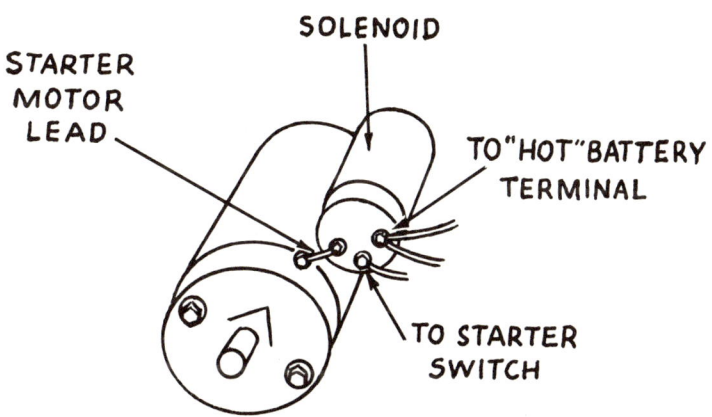

Starter connections.

procedures for electrical equipment as well as procedures for testing assemblies with a voltmeter.

Ignition Check

Troubleshooting the ignition system for a no-start problem involves checking through the primary and secondary ignition circuits from the battery to the spark plugs. Locating the short circuit can be done quickly by following the easy tests below. The initial test for troubleshooting the ignition system was to check for the strength and pulse of the arc between a disconnected spark plug wire to its terminal one-quarter to one-half inch away. A poor spark indicates ignition system trouble.

Testing ignition switch. Ignition switch failures are the most frequent so they should be checked first. Find the wire from the ignition switch that leads to the ignition coil, disconnect it at the coil and turn on the ignition. Touch the detached wire momentarily to a ground. Watch for a faint spark. No spark indicates a failure in the switch or in wiring or connections between the battery and the coil. If the wire did spark when touched to a ground, reconnect it to the coil before proceeding.

Checking coil circuit. Though the coil supplies electrical power to the distributor cap and from there to the spark plugs, it is energized and timed by the contact points inside the distributor. Therefore, checking the coil also requires testing the points.

First remove the distributor cap. Check it and the distributor rotor (on the shaft below the cap) for fractures and worn metal parts. Check the center carbon contact (button) in the distributor cap. The button should extend from the cap, be clean and have no cracks.

Slowly turn the engine by hand (grasping the fan belt and pulley) until the contact points are fully apart. After removing the high-tension coil lead from the distributor cap (center wire), turn on the ignition switch. With a small screwdriver, firmly short-circuit the movable contact point to the fixed contact point while holding the disconnected high-tension wire approximately one-quarter-inch from a ground. Repeated make and break of the circuit with the screwdriver should give an intermittent spark from the high-tension wire to ground. A weak spark, or none at all, means there is a bad ignition coil or faulty wiring between the distributor points and the coil.

Inspection of contact points. While the contact points are still positioned fully apart, make checks to determine if they should be cleaned or replaced or if the condenser is bad.

First, inspect the points for pits and discoloration. Second, with the ignition switched on, firmly slide a screwdriver slowly down the side of the movable contact almost to the base of the distributor. As the screwdriver gets closer, electricity should arc to the base. If there is no spark or the spark is not strong and distinct, the

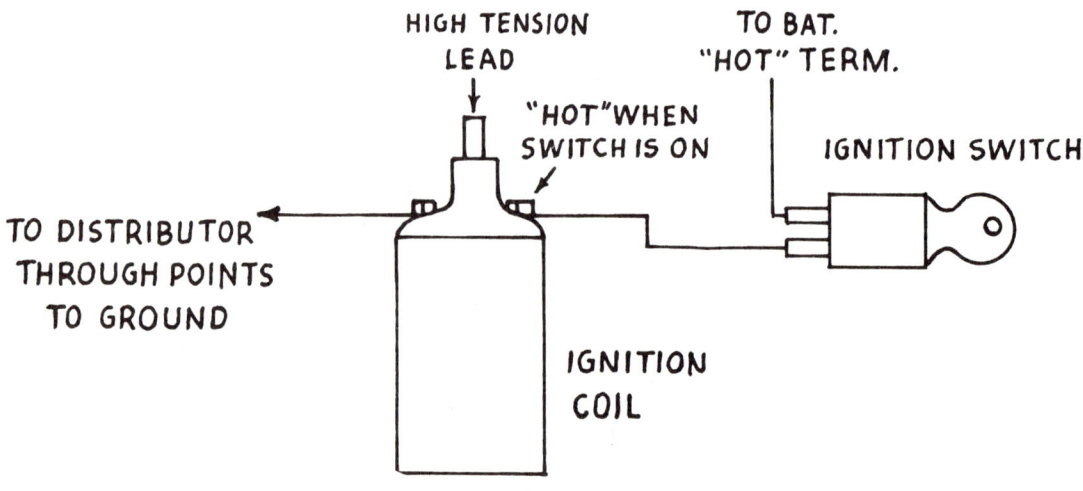

Ignition coil connections.

contaminate breaker points.

Detailed instructions for overhauling the distributor to specifications are given in Chapter Five.

Checking Points, Condenser, Connections

Carefully examine the contact (often called breaker) assemblies in the distributor for the following poor-performance conditions:

1. Points are blackened, pitted, or excessively worn. (Points in extended service normally become dull gray without losing efficiency.)

2. Movable contact-point arm has lost spring action.

3. Fiber rubbing block on breaker is badly worn or loose.

4. Coil primary wire (attached to the breaker assembly with the condenser) is twisted, frayed, or shorted on the distributor plate.

5. Condenser lead connection is loose or damaged.

6. Ground wire (pigtail) between the breaker assembly plate and the distributor housing is frayed or loose.

If any of the distributor components is faulty, replace it and then identify and repair the fault so that the new part can give satisfactory service. Contact points that are slightly burned can be cleaned with a thin cut-stone or point file.

Adjusting point gap. The breaker points must be set correctly before adjusting ignition timing. Turn the crankshaft until a cam lobe on the distributor shaft has fully raised the breaker arm. Loosen the breaker plate hold-down screw and, using a feeler gauge, adjust the breaker gap to the correct setting by canting a screwdriver in the oval cutout. Then tighten the hold-down screw.

Steps for adjusting distributor dwell angle with a dwell meter are listed in Chapter Five.

Coil and polarity. An ignition coil having reversed polarity could reduce spark plug efficiency as much as 20 percent. The result would be a drastic loss of power.

Inspect the coil housing for weak spots and cracks (especially around the tower) cause by high voltage leaks or deterioration.

A check to determine if the ignition polarity matches the battery circuit polarity can easily be made in any of three ways.

1. For negative-to-ground systems, firmly

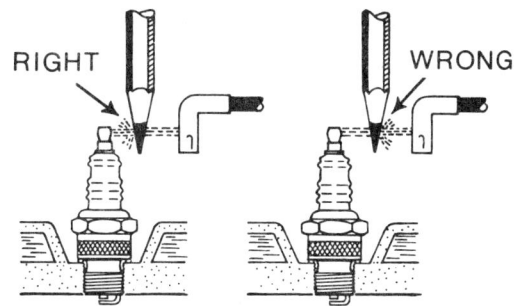

Coil polarity check.

attach a high-reading (few-thousand-volt) voltmeter positive lead to engine ground. (Connect negative to ground for positive-to-ground system) Then momentarily touch the other lead of the voltmeter to the secondary-circuit coil wire that leads to the distributor cap. A positive (up-scale) voltage reading indicates correct polarity. A negative (down-scale) reading shows a reversed polarity that will cause hard starting and premature wear of ignition components.

2. An optional test is to hold a soft-lead wood pencil in the gap between a disconnected spark plug cable and ground. With the engine cranking, observe the direction of spark jump between a disconnected spark plug cable and plug at ground. Flaring of spark between the pencil and ground means that polarity is correct.

3. Dishing on the electrode side indicates wrong polarity. If polarity is wrong, reverse the two primary leads at the ignition coil.

Burning away, or dishing, of side electrode indicates wrong coil polarity.

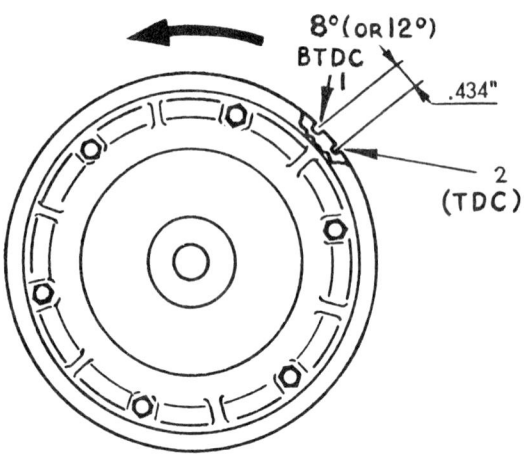

For initial timing of Simca 1000, use pulley mark 1, because the engine turns counterclockwise.

Setting ignition timing. If you have not set the breaker point gap, do so before proceeding. See section, ADJUSTING POINT GAP. Next, turn the crankshaft until top dead center (mark 2) is in line with the oil pump mark (See illustration). The No. 1 piston should be in TDC position. Turn crankshaft so that Mark 1 is in line with the oil pump mark and follow these steps:

a. Remove the rotor arm

b. Loosen the clamp screw at base of distributor body

c. Connect a 12-volt test lamp in series between the distributor primary post and a ground

d. Turn on the ignition

e. Turn distributor body counterclockwise until the light goes out (contacts closed), then turn slowly clockwise until the exact moment the points open and the light goes on again

f. Tighten distributor clamp screw

g. Reinstall rotor arm and distributor cap

h. Check ignition timing with a strobe light (if available) while engine is idling at 600 rpm and all vacuum hoses are disconnected from the distributor and plugged.

Checking Vacuum

The vacuum gauge shows the difference in pressure between the inside and outside of the intake manifold. Since the atmospheric pressure varies with altitude and changes daily with the weather, the action of the vacuum gauge needle is more indic-ative than any specific pressure valve. In general, the vacuum reading is less for higher elevation and also shows a drop from an extreme high-pressure weather system to a stormy, low-pressure system. Pressure measurement is in inches. A well-tuned engine will give a vacuum reading of between 18 and 20 inches at sea level.

Reading a vacuum. Attach the gauge to the intake manifold or on the engine side of the carburetor throttle butterfly. Warm the engine. Set the idle speed between 800 and 1000 rpm, remove the air filter (in case it is partially clogged) and check to see that the carburetor choke is open.

Make the first reading with the engine idling around 900 rpm. The needle should be steady and in the 18-20 inch range. If the pointer remains steady but at a substantially lower pressure, the poor-performance problem affects power in all of the cylinders. It could be improper ignition or valve timing or an intake manifold leak. Improper valve timing normally gives the indicator a lower reading (7-inch drop) than poor ignition timing (4-inch drop). The size of a manifold leak determines where the indicator will stabilize. A severe warp or crack may reduce vacuum as much as 15 inches.

If the vacuum indicator wavers or fluctuates at idle rpm, the poor-performance problem normally affects only one or maybe a few cylinders. Use the illustrated guide to interpret vacuum gauge readings.

Checking Compression

A second important instrument is the compression gauge, used to measure pressure differences among cylinders. Pressure variations cause loss of power and poor idling.

Warm the engine to operating temperature, remove all spark plugs, prop open the throttle linkage so air is not restricted and attach the compression gauge to the spark plug opening.

Crank engine with throttle open and note gauge pointer reading after fifth revolution. Repeat procedure on each cylinder. All cylinders should be within ten pounds of each other and maintain the average pressure given in tune-up specifications.

One or two low readings in the cylinders indicate trouble with valves, rings, pistons, or combustion-chamber leaks. Low com-

	Vacuum Reading	Possible Reasons	Next Test
	Drifts at idle; stabilizes at higher engine rpm.	Burnt valve; combustion chamber leak.	Make compression tests.
	Wavers irregularly in one range despite engine speed.	Unbalanced carburetion; improper spark plug gap, ignition timing; poor valve seating.	Adjust carburetors; check plug gap; check distributor and advance spark; make compression tests.
	Vacuum averages lower than normal at idle, needle fluctuates almost 3″ on both sides of normal.	Worn valve guides admitting air—upsetting carburetion.	Squirt oil on guide seals. Check vacuum improvement.
	Steady gauge reading 18–20″ at all speeds. Throttle is released and engine speed quickly cuts from over 2000 rpm to idle. Needle jumps 2–5″ above normal and then quickly drops to normal without pause or hesitation.	Normal engine performance.	Vacuum okay. Go to compression tests.
	Steady low reading. Figure A. (less than 2″ drop)	Retarded ignition timing.	Loosen clamp, rotate distributor to reset timing. Check gauge improvement.
	Steady, very low reading. Figure B.	Late valve timing.	Check valve timing. Make compression tests.
	Steady, extremely low reading. (up to 15″ drop) Figure C.	Severely warped or cracked intake manifold. Bad carburetor-to-manifold gasket.	Inspect manifold. Squirt oil around seal to detect leak.

	Vacuum Reading	Possible Reasons	Next Test
	Pointer does not jump much above normal when throttle is quickly closed and engine speed is cut from above 2000 rpm to idle. Figure A.	Piston rings may be worn or defective and are blowing into crankcase.	Take compression test of cylinders to pinpoint trouble.
	Pointer jumps 2–5″ above normal upon quick deceleration but hesitates at higher pressure before returning to normal. Figure B.	Restricted exhaust system is causing back-pressure on engine.	Check exhaust for dents, restrictions, clogged muffler.
	Pointer (rhythmically drops 1–7″ below normal vacuum at regular intervals.	Leaking combustion chamber or valve; (ignition or plug failure involving one cylinder).	Make compression tests; (make ignition check).
	Pointer drops rapidly but intermittently (not every time) and then recovers.	Valve sticking at times won't close tight.	Note which valve sticks. Apply penetrating oil to one valve guide at a time. Problem will correct itself temporarily.
	Pointer wavers rapidly between 10–20″ at idle becoming worse with higher rpm.	Weak or broken spring causing valve to close slowly.	Remove valve covers; check condition of springs.
	Wavers irregularly at idle; fluctuates rapidly in smaller range at higher rpm.	Manifold leak at intake port—upsets and reduces cylinder draft.	Squirt oil around manifold; check vacuum increase when oil fills leak. Replace faulty gasket.

pression readings in all cylinders indicate incorrect valve timing. To determine the fault, squirt about an ounce of light oil into the low-compression cylinder, replace the compression gauge, and crank the engine another five revolutions for the second reading. If compression increases substantially, the rings are worn or stuck and need replacing.

No increase in compression after adding oil to the cylinder narrows the trouble to improper valve seating, a cracked or broken piston, or a combustion-chamber leak between the head and the cylinder.

First, check out the possibility of a combustion-chamber leak. Turn the engine while checking for hissing noises and perhaps a discharge of oil from the flange between the cylinder and the head. This indicates a poor seal between the cylinder head and the cylinder. A leaky head gasket can often be detected by loss of compression in two adjacent cylinders.

Detecting piston damage involves replacing all the spark plugs, starting the engine, and listening for a distinctive clicking noise at idle and upon acceleration. Combustion gases (blow-by) will also escape into the crankcase through the piston crack. See TROUBLESHOOTING ENGINE NOISES, in this chapter.

Abnormal Oil Consumption

Another way to identify poor-performance troubles is to check oil consumption. Continual addition of oil, fouled spark plugs, and blue-gray exhaust smoke are obvious signs of excessive oil consumption.

Worn or broken piston rings permit oil to enter the combustion chamber and reduce burning efficiency. In addition, poor rings permit combustion gases to enter the crankcase. This hot blow-by changes the crankcase oil into vapor that escapes through the ventilating system. Blow-by, if excessive, could also pressurize the crankcase, forcing oil leakage through weak pan seals.

Worn valve guides fail to keep oil out of the combustion chamber, resulting in poor performance and excessive oil consumption.

Before assuming that engine wear is the cause of excessive oil usage, make a thorough inspection for external leaks. After placing clean paper underneath the engine, run it at a medium speed until the oil is hot. Stop the engine and check for oil drippings on the paper. Trace the leak to its source and correct it. In many cases the leak is the sole cause of abnormal oil consumption. It's been estimated that a single drop of oil lost every 50 feet will amount to a full quart every 500 miles, an amount worth saving.

Greater oil consumption is normal if the oil used is too light or if the engine is run often at high speed. A break-in period for new rings also requires additional oil.

High Ring Friction

In a newly rebuilt engine, poor performance is sometimes due to too much ring friction. Firm expander springs often press the rings too tightly against the cylinder walls. Engine power and gas economy drop conspicuously.

Test for excessive ring friction by holding the throttle open to an engine speed of 1000 rpm. Then turn off the ignition. An engine with proper tension will slow to a stop and then roll back and forth momentarily. An engine with tight rings will stop suddenly without rolling.

Adjusting Valve Clearance

Improper valve clearance adjustment results in loss of power and possible valve damage. Excessive clearance can be detected by noisy valves. Insufficient clearance causes valves to burn and possible backfiring through the carburetor.

When the engine is at operating temperature, remove the air cleaner and rocker cover. Turn the engine over by hand until the pushrod stops falling. The valve is fully closed at this point.

Basic valve-clearance adjustment for each cylinder is at the point where both valves are closed—TDC of the piston's compression stroke. Follow the firing order of the engine, which is 1-3-4-2. Final adjustment of all valves is when the engine is at operating temperature and slowly idling.

Troubleshooting Engine Noises

If engine noises can be located and analyzed before the engine is disassembled, correcting the problem is much easier. However, fine tuning is not possible until mechanical engine troubles are repaired. For locating noises, a piece of water hose of convenient length is a handy substitute for a stethoscope.

Valve noises. Valve noise is a loud rhythmic clicking that varies directly with rpm but occurs at half the beat of other engine noises because the camshaft rotates at half engine speed.

Remove the valve covers to help locate noises better. Set engine rpm to the speed where the noise is most pronounced. If needed, hold the end of a piece of hose one-half inch from tappets, and listen to one valve at a time until the noisemaker is identified.

Sticky valves and tappets with excessive clearance have similar sounds, although sticking-valve noises are normally intermittent. Check for excessive tappet clearance by inserting a feeler gauge between the noisy valve stem and its tappet. If the noise stops, reset the clearance. Valves will burn if clearance is reduced below factory specifications. Valve sticking becomes pronounced when the engine idles after having been run hard. As the idling engine cools to its normal operating temperature the sticking-valve noise lessens. When a valve sticks, the lost compression from improper closing makes the engine idle roughly.

Warped and burnt valves also cause the engine to run irregularly, especially under low-speed load. They sometimes click but more often make hissing, wheezing sounds through the exhaust manifold (exhaust valve) or backfire (intake valve) through the carburetor.

Broken springs and bent valve stems don't close valves properly and are noisy as well.

Loose rocker arms, and bent or worn pushrods, transmit heavy rattling sounds.

Piston noises. Generally, piston noises result from a piston slapping from side to side on its bore due to excessive clearance. However, if the piston noise is faint in a cold engine and disappears shortly after the engine reaches operating temperature, the condition might not be worth special attention.

Individual piston noises can be detected by shorting out one spark plug at a time while the engine is under partial load until the noises ceases. The piston makes no noise when its spark plug doesn't fire.

A collapsed or badly worn piston makes a low-pitched, dull metallic noise when the engine is under a load.

Broken rings or a cylinder ridge not removed when installing new rings will produce a steady, clicking, metallic noise at all engine speeds.

Loose wrist pins give a sharp metallic knock that is more noticeable when the engine is idling. Speeding up the engine to about 1500 rpm and then releasing the throttle is another way to detect the wrist pin knock.

Crankshaft bearing noises. Crankshaft noises can be grouped into main bearing noise, connecting rod noise, and crankshaft end-play noise.

A loose main bearing gives a heavy bumping noise when the engine is under load. A loose connecting rod bearing has a steady rap after letting up slightly on the accelerator when car is driven about 50 mph.

Shorting one spark plug at a time relieves pressure on each connecting rod bearing in turn and thereby deadens the noise of the defective bearing.

Excessive crankshaft end-play can be

Piston damaged by inaudible detonation and pre-ignition at high speeds.

heard as a thud each time the clutch pedal is depressed.

A rasping noise, when speeding and slowing the engine, indicates a loose fly wheel.

Detonation. Detonation, an explosion rather than a smooth burning of the fuel in a cylinder, is caused by an imbalance of compression, heat, fuel, valves, and timing. Detonation can be devastating to engine parts.

Each of the following problems must be eliminated to prevent detonation.

1. Excessive cooling system temperature.
2. Insufficient spark plug heat range.
3. Over-advanced ignition timing.
4. Too-low fuel octane rating.
5. Lean carburetor/fuel mixture.
6. Stuck manifold heat control valve.

With the ignition system checked, the vacuum and compression readings interpreted, and engine noises investigated, the mechanic should have a good indication of any mechanical defects in the engine. These malfunctions should be corrected before attempting to tune the engine. Detailed overhaul procedures for the ignition system and engine mechanical parts are provided in later chapters.

Cleaning Fuel System

A final pre-tune-up step involves cleaning the carburetors, fuel filters and, if necessary, lines and tank.

Many fuel system problems result from accumulation of water, dirt, and gummy residues in the tank, lines, and pump. Other problems are caused by restricted tank ventilation, leaky lines and connections, and worn out moving parts. These troubles, when identified before disassembly, can be eliminated efficiently.

Ideally, the carburetor should be taken apart, cleaned thoroughly, and reassembled with new gasketing and other non-metal parts. If complete disassembly is not feasible, it is recommended that the carburetor jets be removed from time to time and blown through with compressed air. Wash carburetor housing with gasoline (engine cold) to remove dirt. Remove only one jet at a time for cleaning to prevent a mistake on replacement.

NOTE: the jets should not be cleaned with a sharp or abrasive object that might cause deformation of the close factory calibration.

Checking fuel-air mixtures. Poor engine performance can be caused by fuel-air mixtures that are either too rich or too lean. Both are harmful to the engine. A lean mixture at high speeds overheats the combustion chambers to the point where the valves might burn. A rich mixture washes lubricating oil from the cylinders, resulting in scuffed rings and scored cylinder walls.

Rub paper or cloth around the inside of the exhaust pipe, checking for carbon deposits. A rich mixture leaves a black residue.

Choke off the carburetor while the warmed engine is running at 1500 rpm. (The palm of the hand can be used to restrict incoming air.) By reducing the air flow, the air-fuel mixture is normally enriched and the engine speeds up somewhat. If it doesn't speed up at all, the mixture adjustment is too rich; if it speeds up drastically, the mixture adjustment is too lean.

When a carburetor has a lean mixture, the engine pauses and then accelerates poorly with apparent sponginess (there might be backfiring). If a weak fuel pump or restricted gas line is the cause of the lean mixture, the engine runs out of fuel at higher engine speeds.

Rich mixture can be caused by high fuel pressure forcing the needle valve from its seat. The carburetor floods and performance breaks down.

A malfunctioning carburetor cannot be tuned and should be overhauled.

Adjusting the Carburetor

Feeding of engine at idle speed is controlled by the jet (g). Richness of idle speed mixture is adjusted by the volume screw (W), allowing a very precise adjustment of engine. Air intake is through a calibrated orifice located in the body of the carburetor in a recessed space beneath the venturi (K).

The engine must be warm, and the spark plugs and points in good condition.

With the engine idling:

1. Slightly tighten throttle stop screw (Z) to increase the speed of the engine
2. Loosen volume control screw (W) until engine begins to idle roughly. Then tighten screw slowly until engine idles smoothly
3. Slowly loosen stop screw (Z) to adjust engine idle to approximately 620 rpm.

NOTE: never completely tighten the volume control screw (W).

Cleaning fuel filters. Loosen the cover retaining screw and remove the screen from the mechanical fuel pump. Wash screen and cover in solvent and blow dry with air. Replace gasket if necessary and reinstall screen, cover and bolt. Then start engine and check for leaks.

Cleaning air filters. To clean the dry paper filter, remove and tap lightly to loosen dirt, or blow out with compressed air. Restricted filters wil adversely affect engine performance. If too dirty, replace the element.

Oil-wetted, metal-mesh air filters can be washed in solvent. Blow out with compressed air or let dry in open. Re-oil lightly prior to installation.

Cleaning carburetor parts. All carburetors have numerous small passages that can be fouled by carbon and gummy deposits. Metal parts should be soaked in carburetor solvent until thooughly clean. However, the solvent will weaken or destroy cork, plastic, and leather components. These parts should be wiped with a clean, lint-free cloth.

While the carburetor is disassembled, check the bowl cover with a straight edge for warped surfaces.

The needle valves and seats should be closely inspected for wear and damage. Replace these parts when imperfect, because their performance critically affects engine tuning.

After cleaning the parts, blow air through the high and low speed jets to ensure that all passages are clear.

Reassemble the carburetor, using new gaskets and other non-metal parts.

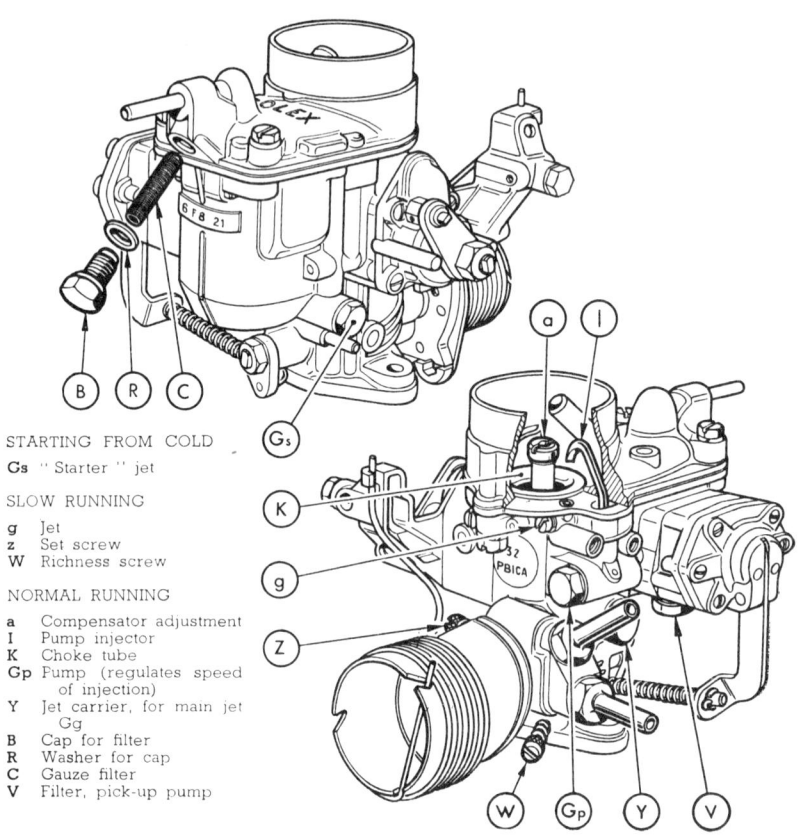

STARTING FROM COLD
Gs " Starter " jet

SLOW RUNNING
g   Jet
z   Set screw
W Richness screw

NORMAL RUNNING
a   Compensator adjustment
I   Pump injector
K   Choke tube
Gp Pump (regulates speed
      of injection)
Y   Jet carrier, for main jet
      Gg
B   Cap for filter
R   Washer for cap
C   Gauze filter
V   Filter, pick-up pump

Solex carburetor parts and adjustments.

Lubricating carburetor linkage. Lubricate all pivot points with one-two drops of engine oil while moving throttle controls. Lubricate accelerator pump rods. Disconnect all ball joints, fill cups with grease, and reconnect. Move linkage back and forth to check for proper functioning.

Clutch Troubleshooting

Clutch slippage, chatter, and grabbing are most noticeable when accelerating from a standstill in first or reverse gears.

Dragging of the clutch is obvious when shifting between gears, especially into and out of reverse.

Dragging—fails to release completely
a. Excessive linkage free play
b. Sticking or faulty pilot bearing
c. Damaged clutch plates (pressure and/ or driven)
d. Release yoke off pivot ball-stud

e. Driven-plate hub binding on main drive gear spline.

Slipping—does not firmly engage
a. Insufficient linkage free play
b. Oil-soaked driven disc (correct oil leak before installing new assembly)
c. Worn or damaged driven disc
d. Warped pressure plate or flywheel
e. Weak diaphragm spring (replace cover assembly)
f. Driven plate not seated (make 20–50 normal starts)
g. Driven plate overheated (check lash after cooled).

Grabbing-chatter—intermittent seizing and slipping
a. Oil spotted, burned, or glazed facings
b. Worn splines on main drive gear or clutch disc
c. Loose engine or drive train mountings
d. Warped pressure plate, clutch disc or flywheel
e. Burned or smeared resin on flywheel or pressure plate (sand smooth if super-

ficial, replace if burned or heat-checked).

Rattling—transmission click

a. Release yoke and leave loose on pivot ball-stud or in bearing groove (replace if necessary)

b. Oil in driven-disc damper (replace driven-disc)

c. Driven-disc damper spring failure (replace driven-disc).

Throw-out bearing noise—clutch fully engaged

a. Improper linkage adjustment

b. Throw-out bearing binding on transmission bearing retainer (clean, lubricate, check for burrs. nicks)

c. Insufficient tension between release yoke and pivot ball-stud (yoke improperly installed and/or linkage spring weak).

Tight pedal—when depressed or returns sluggishly

a. Bind in linkage (lubricate and free up)

b. Weak pressure plate spring

c. Weak linkage spring

d. Driven disc worn.

Transmission Troubleshooting

Noise—in forward speeds

a. Low lubricant level or incorrect lubricant

b. Transmission misaligned or loose

c. Mainshaft bearing or front main bearing worn or damaged

d. Countergear or bearings worn or damaged

e. Main drive gear or synchronizers worn or damaged.

Noise—in reverse

a. Reverse sliding gear or shaft, worn or damaged.

Hard shifting

a. Clutch improperly adjusted

b. Shift shafts or forks worn

c. Incorrect lubricant

d. Synchronizers worn or broken.

Jumping out of gear

a. Partial engagement of gear

b. Transmission misaligned or loose

c. Worn pilot bearing

d. End-play in main drive gear (bearing retainer loose or broken, loose or worn bearings on main drive gear and mainshaft)

e. Worn clutch teeth on main drive gear and/or on synchronizer sleeve

f. Worn or broken blocking rings

g. Bent mainshaft.

Sticking in gear

a. Clutch not released fully

b. Low lubricant level or incorrect lubrication

c. Defective (tight) main drive gear pilot bearing

d. Frozen blocking ring on main drive gear cone

e. Burred or battered teeth on synchronizer sleeve and/or main drive gear.

Front End Troubleshooting

When servicing steering and front suspension assemblies, it is advisable to check every front end part, because all of the assemblies are so closely interrelated.

First, check the front end for worn or loose-fitting parts. Repair or replace what is faulty. Second, inspect and adjust the steering gear assembly. Third, set the front end alignment. And fourth, balance the wheels.

To detect front-end troubles quickly, follow these simple procedures:

1. With the front end jacked up, shake both wheels simultaneously to detect any looseness between them. Tie-rod and steering linkage joints sometimes loosen under severe road stresses. Check weaknesses further by oscillating and prying against members connected to these joints.

2. Check out wheel suspension joints by having each wheel shaken up and down while the steering knuckle and control arm joints are observed for play.

3. Spin the wheels rapidly to test for deteriorated bearings. Listen for bearing noise and touch the bumper to feel vibration that rough bearings create.

4. Rig a piece of chalk so it just clears the wheel rim, then rotate the wheel to test for wheel runout. The chalk will mark misaligned, protruding rim areas. Repeat test on inside rim. Wheel should be straightened if runout exceeds one-eighth inch.

5. Lower front end to ground and rebound fenders to check for deteriorated shock absorbers.

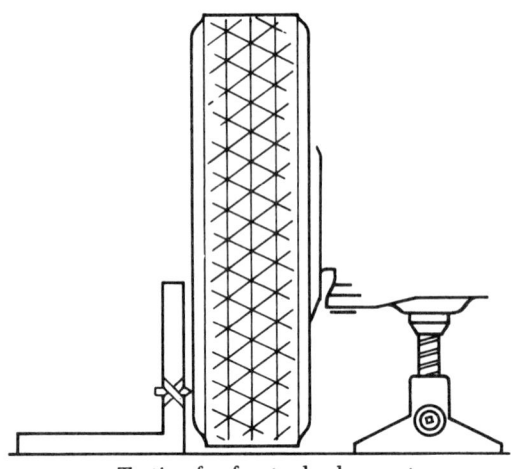

Testing for front wheel runout.

6. Check pre-owned cars for possible front end damage by measuring and comparing the wheelbase on both sides. Measure carefully from common points such as from the rear of the front-wheel rim to the rear of the back-wheel rim. If one side has a shorter or longer wheelbase than is listed in specifications, compare several measurements on both sides between various points until the dislocated part is found.

Diagonal measurements from right front to left rear wheels and from left front to right rear wheels will uncover a distorted chassis (if wheelbase measurements are equal). A twisted chassis will alter tracking and make front end alignment difficult if not impossible.

Vehicle Wandering

Vehicle wandering is annoying and dangerous and requires constant steering wheel correction. It may be caused by incorrect caster or toe-in, too-low tire pressure, excessive or insufficient play in the steering mechanism, worn or stiff steering rod ball joints, stiff control arm system, excessive play in rear end suspension.

Pulling to one Side

Check for uneven tire pressure, weak or uneven front springs, stiff wheel bearing, faulty wheel alignment, dragging brake, bent steering rod, or incorrect camber.

Hard Steering

Caused by too-low tire pressure, insufficiently lubricated steering gears or front end, excessive caster, damaged bearing in gear housing or steering column, damaged thrust bearing in steering knuckles, damaged front axle member or body.

Shimmy

Wheels bent, misaligned or unbalanced, worn or warped brake drum, too-low tire pressure, damaged steering rod, loose or worn front wheel bearings.

Front End Alignment

Front end alignment centers on the precise geometric relationship of a number of parts—even when they are changing positions—that provides front wheel stability and control. These geometric angles include steering axis cant, caster, camber, included angle, toe-in, and toe-out (turning arc).

Before any adjustment is made, the condition of the complete front-end system should be checked following the procedures given in the previous paragraphs and any defects corrected. Check the air pressure in all the tires. Check that the front tires are worn evenly. If not, replace or rotate them with the rear tires. Front wheel alignment must always be adjusted in this order: caster, camber, and toe-in. The

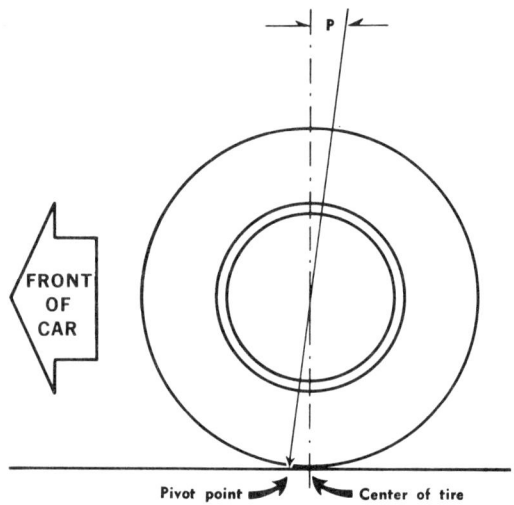

Front wheel caster. P=positive caster. The pivot point ahead of the center line of the tire holds the wheel stable.

methods used in making these adjustments are described in Chapter Seven.

Caster. Caster is the cant of the upper ball joint toward the rear of the car (positive). It gives the wheel another type of directional stability by moving the pivot point of the wheel forward of the tire's center. Positioning the pivot point ahead of center causes a drag on the bottom of the wheel (at the center) when it turns, thereby resisting the turn and tending to hold the wheel steady in whatever direction it has been going.

Too slight a caster angle will cause the wheels to wander or weave at high speed and steer erratically when the brakes are applied. Too great a caster angle creates hard steering and shimmy at low speeds.

Camber. Camber is the angle that the centerline of the wheel makes with the vertical. The top of the wheel cants away from the car so that the center of the tire at the road lies at a point projected along the inclined axis of the upper and lower ball joints (steering axis cant). Placing the weight of the car directly over the pivot point allow easiest steering and takes some load off the outside wheel bearing.

Toe-out. Toe-out (turning arc) is the difference in angle of the two wheels in a turn. As the front end turns, the outside wheel describes a larger circle than does the inside wheel. The turning angle of each is, therefore, not the same and the difference of the two angles is toe-out. If all previously discussed front end angles and measurements are correct and yet toe-out is wrong, one, or both, of the steering arms is bent.

Toe-in. Usually measured in inches, this is the amount that both wheels are closer together at the front than at the rear. Toe-in is related to wheel camber and compression forces on the steering linkage with forward speed. The greater the camber, the greater is the toe-in, usually. Set toe-in only after checking caster and camber.

Steering axis cant. Steering axis cant, or kingpin inclination, is the angle (from the vertical) at which the steering knuckle is attached to the upper and lower ball joints. The canted steering knuckle controls wheel directional stability by forcing the wheel to lift the chasis in order to turn from a straight ahead direction. As the steering arm releases its force over the wheel, the wheel returns to its straight ahead position under the force of the chassis weight. This inclination is not adjustable.

Included angle. This is found by adding the steering axis cant to the positive wheel camber. This total must be equal on both front wheels regardless of what individual differences exist in axis cant and camber between the wheels. If the included angles of the two sides are different, a wheel spindle might be bent, possibly from striking a curb sharply.

Engine

Simca 1204

The power unit for the Simca 1204 is a four-cylinder, 69 cu. in. engine mounted in a transverse position in the front of the car and tilted 41°. Crankshaft rotation is counterclockwise when facing the engine at the front near the flywheel. Premium fuel is recommended for the GL and GLS models with a compression ratio of 9.6 to 1. The LS model has a compression ratio of 8.2 to 1 and uses regular fuel.

Power Unit Removal

The power unit is removed as follows: place the car on a lift, remove hood, disconnect battery and raise lift.

From under car, disconnect starter solenoid wires and remove alternator belt cover. Drain cooling system by removing water pump drain screw. Remove clutch slave cylinder, but do not disconnect fluid feed line. Temporarity fasten cylinder to front grille. Remove exhaust pipe flange and disconnect gear shift linkage and selector cable near transmission. Detach speedometer cable from axle housing.

Remove engine rear bracket from lower

Engine Specifications

Car Model	Cyl.	Displacement Cu. In./CC.	Nom. Bore In./MM.	Stroke In./MM.	Compression Ratio	Torque Ft. Lbs./ KGM/RPM	BHP/RPM (SAE)	No. Main Bearings
1000 Sedan	4	57.6/944	2.67/68	2.55/65	7.8:1	54.24/7.5/2800	45/5000	5
1000 Coupe	4	57.6/944	2.67/68	2.55/65	9.2:1	54.97/7.6/3500	52/3500	5
1204 GL, GLS	4	69/1120	2.9/74	2.55/65	9.6:1	56.4/7.8/3600	53/5800	5
1204 LS	4	69/1120	2.9/74	2.55/65	8.2:1	60/8.3/3600	56/5800	5
Simca 5	4	78.7/1290	2.9/74	2.95/75	8.5:1	72.8/10.1/2500	65/5200	
1118	4	68.2/1118	2.9/74	2.55/65	9.0:1	56.5/7.9/2600	56/5600	5

same holes. Separate transmission-front axle assembly from engine by disassembling clutch housing from cylinder block.

Remove warm air intake and rocker arm cover. Remove cylinder head attaching screw near exhaust and screw in lifting eyebolt. Attach pedestal adapter plate to cylinder block. Lift engine with a hoist, and attach adapter plate to disassembly pedestal.

With engine on pedestal, disconnect spark plug cable, wire and vacuum line from distributor. Remove and place on bench: engine oil dipstick and bracket; distributor and mounting flange; fuel pump and insulating plate; engine oil breather plug and line to be disconnected from carburetor; carburetor; water outlet elbow cap and thermostat; water outlet elbow on cylinder head; water inlet pipe on oil pan; water manifold; oil distributor bracket and drive bushing; and intake manifold.

Remove water pump pulley and belt. Remove hose connecting water pump to timing gear cover. Remove water pump, exhaust manifold, oil filter, plug of discharge valve, valve body, spring and ball, oil pump cover, oil pump body and gears.

Remove spark plugs and temperature feeler. Loosen locknuts of rocker arm adjusting screws. Remove cylinder head mounting screws in reverse of tightening order (see illustration). Remove rocker arm and shaft assembly after it has been retained with tool PN20863T. Remove pushrods, marking them for reassembly in the same order. Remove cylinder head. Install

flywheel ring gear retaining tool. Place cylinder block vertical with flywheel facing upwards. Punch-mark clutch mechanism to index with flywheel, and remove clutch and plate. Turn block so that oil pan faces up and remove the oil pan extension, oil exhaust strainer and oil pan. Place block vertical and remove crankshaft pulley, timing gear cover and engine support plate. Remove cam shaft driven wheel and timing chain. Remove crankshaft wheel with hammer and wood drift or with puller PN15525F and plate SIVA.

Remove distributor gear after prying retaining ring up and out of oil pump driving shaft groove. Push oil pump driving shaft with a screwdriver and remove through other face. Remove camshaft. Loosen, but do not remove, six flywheel mounting screws. Remove flywheel ring gear retaining tool. Turn cylinder block over and remove connecting rod big end caps, placing nylon covers on cap screws. Set crankshaft to upper or lower dead center, remove carbon deposits, then remove rod and piston assemblies. Reassemble big end caps to proper rods. Remove connecting rod bearings and mark for proper reassembly.

Set block vertical and remove flywheel and front seal shell. Remove crankshaft. Remove all bearings and half thrust washers and place in order. Install crankshaft main bearing caps but do not tighten screws. Remove adjusting bushings from the front sealing shell, clutch housing, cylinder head and timing gear cover.

Engine Assembly

Installing crankshaft. Remove bearing caps from the cylinder block and wipe half-shells clean. Place bearings in their proper places.

NOTE: shells of main bearings 2 and 4 have a center oil groove, others do not. Also, shells of main bearing 3 are wider.

Lubricate half-thrust washers with grease and apply on main bearing webs, babitted side out. Wipe crankpins and journals clean and oil each half-bearing shell. Install crankshaft evenly on five main bearings. Check proper setting of half-thrust washers. Install main bearing caps in their proper positions, with marks facing each other and visible from the camshaft side of the engine. Tighten screws at correct

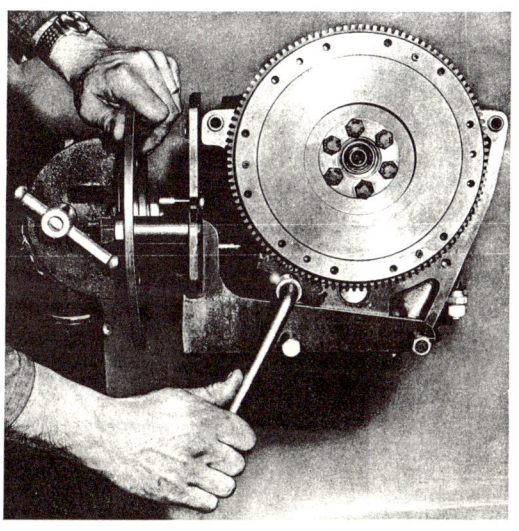

Installing locking tool on flywheel ring gear.

Crankshaft, Camshaft and Connecting Rod Specifications

Car Model	CRANKSHAFT			CAMSHAFT JOURNALS			CONNECTING RODS		
	Main Journals In./MM Dia.	Rod Journals In./MM Dia.	End Play In./MM	Front In./MM Dia.	Middle In./MM Dia.	Rear In./MM Dia.	Big End Bore In./MM	Small End Bore In./MM	Weight Tolerance Ozs/Gr
1000	1.89/ 47.9	1.49/ 38.0	.005–.010/.12–.27	1.39/ 35.5	1.43/ 36.5	1.47/ 37.5	1.62/ 41.0	.82/20.9	∓.105/3
1204			.003–.010/.09–.27	1.39/ 35.5	1.60/ 40.9	1.63/ 41.4	1.73/ 44.0	.87/22.0	
Simca 5	1.77/ 44.0	1.73/ 44.0	.003–.010/.09–.27					.87/22.0	

torque, starting with the center cap.

Crankshaft bearing clearances should range from .0016 to .0029 in. (.04–.07 mm.) and connecting rod clearances from .0012 to .0025 in. (.03–.06 mm.). These clearances can be measured by use of Plastigages. The measurement must be performed on clean, oil-free parts. Crankshaft lateral clearance is measured with a dial micrometer or feeler gauges while moving the crankshaft lengthwise with a screwdriver.

Seat ball bearing with tool PN20874W and install the two adjusting bushings of the front shell. Apply lubricated paper gasket on block, oil the sealing ring lip and fit shell, by pushing ring lip. Torque screws with lockwashers. Smooth off any part of paper gasket that protrudes from bearing edge.

Install flywheel being sure to include thrush washer.

NOTE: mounting holes are not symmetrical so only one position on the crankshaft is possible.

Install connecting rod and piston assemblies in cylinders with piston marks toward engine rear (away from flywheel) and rod marks toward camshaft. Oil crankpins and cylinders and fit nylon caps to rod cap screws. Set rings with gaps 120° apart. Fit connecting rod big end caps with notches of half shells facing each other. Tighten to specified torque. Check that there is no drag when turning the crankshaft. Check connecting rod big end lateral clearance on each crankpin, which should range from .003 to .010 in. (.10–.27 mm.).

Installing camshaft. Set block vertical, timing gear face up. Install two adjustment bushings in block. Oil camshaft journals, then fit camshaft in block. Install

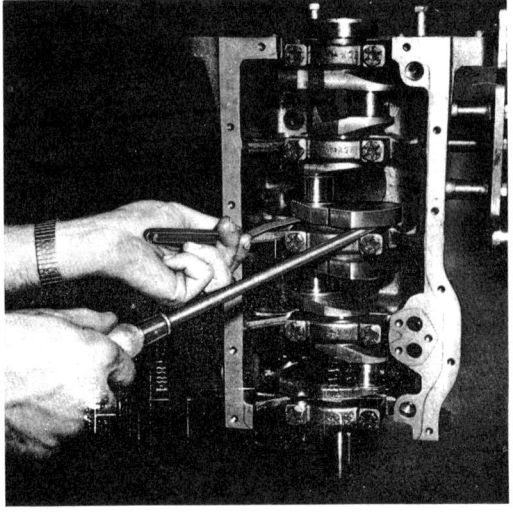

Measuring crankshaft end play.

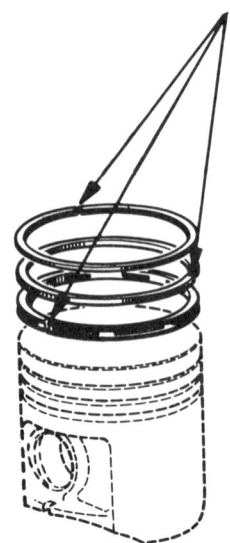

Set piston rings with gaps 120° apart.

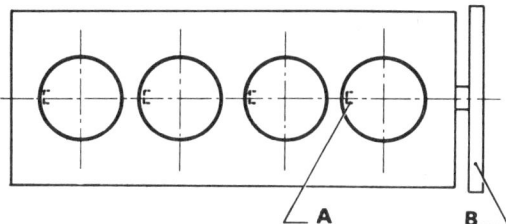

Install pistons with marks toward rear.

Positioning of timing gears.

Installing Truarc ring.

locating flange, sliding it in camshaft third journal groove. Tighten screws at specified torque and peen retainers. With a screwdriver, move camshaft lengthwise and measure play with a dial micrometer or feeler gauges. The play should range from .003 to .007 in. (.10–.20 mm.).

Timing gear installation. Set piston No. 1 (cylinder nearest flywheel) at upper dead center. Fit retaining pin of crankshaft sprocket wheel. Install wheels and timing chain on crankshaft and camshaft, timing marks facing each other. Turn crankshaft until three holes of drive wheel match three holes of crankshaft (only one such position is possible). Install screws and tighten to specified torque. Lubricate timing gear cover gasket, apply to block and install timing gear cover. Install right-hand engine bracket and tighten. Install crankshaft pulley and tighten to specified torque.

Installing oil pump drive shaft. Lubricate oil pump drive shaft and install in cylinder block. Fit distributor drive gear to camshaft worm gear.

NOTE: the pinion bore is not tapered along its entire length. The untapered, grooved end must be placed first.

Lubricate side face of pinion. Apply Truarc ring on pinion face and with a screwdriver, push ring to lower it in shaft groove. Lateral clearance should range from .001 to .019 in. (.05–.50 mm.).

Install oil pan and oil strainer by lubricating strainer seal and oil pan gasket and applying to the cylinder block. Position oil pan, attach with 14 screws and tighten at proper torque. Attach oil strainer. Lubricate oil pan extension gasket and mount oil

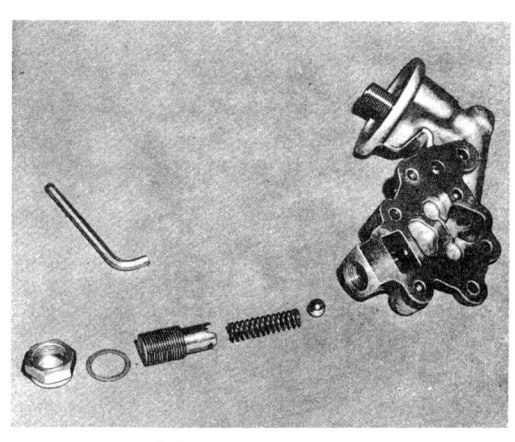

Oil pump components.

pan extension with gasket and 16 screws. Tighten to proper torque.

Install water pump with cylinder block in vertical position. Lubricate pump seal, and attach seal and pump to oil pan with four screws. Tighten drain plug and seal on pump. Tighten all screws at specified torque.

Install oil pump body with lubricated seal on cylinder block. Fit driven gear in body, turning slowly until shaft slots mesh. Install valve seat, ball, spring, and valve body in cover, and attach cover with cement-coated gasket. Attach pump assembly to cylinder block, and tighten screws and valve body at specified torque. Tighten plug and seal, and screw in threaded tube that holds filter. Attach filter element with gasket and hand tighten.

Cylinder head installation. Oil and install eight pushrods. With a mallet, fit two head-adjusting bushings on block. Oil head gasket and place on block with marking up. Install head and drive eight rocker arm rods through holes. Assemble rocker arms and shafts.

CAUTION: one end of shaft is drilled. Set drilled end outward. There is a front shaft and a rear shaft.

Drive rocker arm shafts through intermediate brackets and install a pin in each bracket. Assemble rocker arms, springs and brackets. Line up the brackets and hold the assembly with tool PN20863T. Place assembly on cylinder head with each bracket on the adjusting bushing. Turn each cylinder head screw a few turns and remove retaining flange. Tighten cylinder head screws a few turns at a time and in the correct sequence, finally to the proper torque.

Install distributor after turning flywheel so that No. 1 cylinder is at ignition point. (intake opens BTDC, fourth cylinder). Set distributor rotor to fire on No. 1 plug wire. Install distributor drive bushing on oil pump drive shaft, with slot aligned with boss on distributor shaft, and distributor positioned with vacuum diaphragm toward rear of engine. Install distributor.

Clutch installation. Position block with flywheel up and install three pins. Position plate and clutch mechanism on flywheel, marks facing each other. Adjust clutch plate with tool PN20870E. Tighten screws gradually at specified torque.

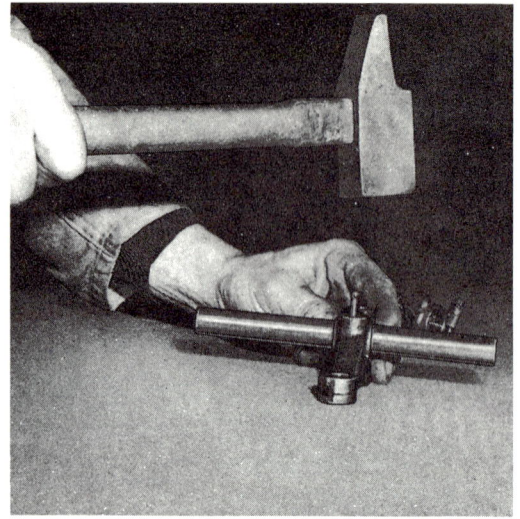

Installing rocker arm bracket pin.

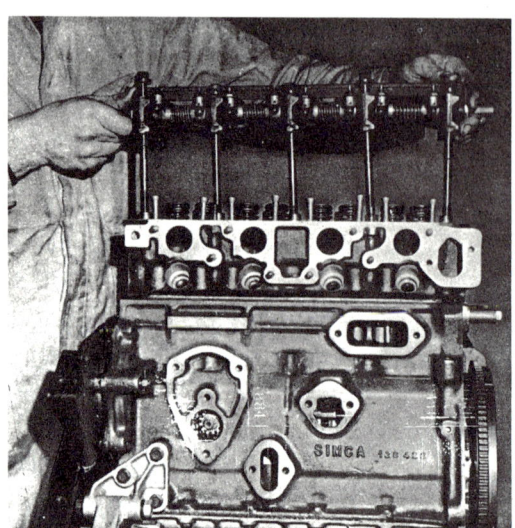

Installing rocker arms and shaft.

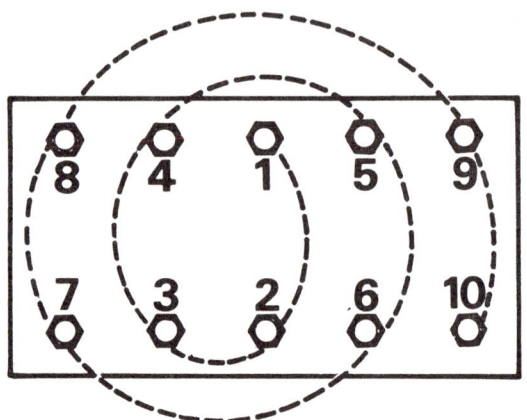

Cylinder head tightening sequence.

Installing distributor drive bushing.

Installing line from fuel pump to carburetor.

CAUTION: length of screws should not exceed .49 in. (12.5 mm.), washer included, or they may touch the ring gear.

Complete engine assembly by installing, in sequence, exhaust manifold, water manifold, carburetor, fuel pump, and miscellaneous items such as spark plugs, oil pressure sensor, thermostat, water drain plug. Install distributor cap and vacuum line and adjust firing point as described in Chapter Five.

Rocker Arm Adjustment

Adjust rocker arms by successively balancing the valves of the opposing cylinder:

Adjust Rocker Arms of Cylinder	Balance Rocker Arms of Cylinder
1	4
2	3
3	2
4	1

Adjust each clearance so that feeler passes with a very slight drag.

Rocker arm clearances:

	Intake	Exhaust
Cold	.011 in. (.30 mm.)	.013 in. (.35 mm.)
Hot	.015 in. (.40 mm.)	.013 in. (.35 mm.)

Piston Pin Removal

Run drift through piston, screw on pilot and place piston on anvil PN20869H so that two flats of anvil do not touch edges of piston grooves. Push drift pin through piston with a hydraulic press.

Rocker arm adjustment.

Piston and Rod Assembly

Heat small end of connecting rod to 428°-482°F (220°–250°C) in hot oil or an electric furnace. Fit new piston pin to drift, screw on pilot and lock. (Do not allow pin to protrude from pilot). Oil piston pin and pilot, and place piston on anvil, pin hole being adjusted on retractable guide. With asbestos glove place heated rod in piston and slide drift fitted with new pin through piston and rod until it touches anvil bottom. If pin protrudes from sides of bosses, adjust length with a hydraulic press.

Valve Specifications

Car Model	Rocker Arm Clearance Hot (H); Cold (C) In./MM.		Head Diameter In./MM.		Stem Diameter In./MM.		Stem Clearance In Guide In./MM.		Spring Length Under Load of 46.3 Lbs. (21 KG) In./MM.	Intake Opens °BTDC
	Int.	Exh.	Int.	Exh.	Int.	Exh.	Int.	Exh.	In./MM.	
1000	.014/ .35(H) .012– .014/ .3– .35(C)	.014/.35(H) .012–.014/ .3–.35(C)	1.14/29	1.02/26	.276/7.0	.275/6.7			1.14/29	16.5
1204	.015/ .39 (H) .011/ .30 (C)	.013/.35(H) .013/.35(C)	1.29/33	1.10/28	.31/7.9	.31/7.9				
Simca 5	.004/ .10 (C)	.006/.15(C)			.32/8.0	.32/8.0	.002/.05	.003/.07		12

Block, Piston and Ring Specifications

Car Model	Class "A" Cyl. Bore In./MM.	Class "A" Piston Dia. At Skirt In./MM.	PISTON PIN Dia. In./MM.	PISTON PIN Fit in Piston In./MM.	Ring Height In./MM.	Ring Clearance in Groove In./MM.	Ring End Gap In./MM.
1000	2.677–2.678/ 67.992–68.002	2.674–2.6745/ 67.935–67.945	.749/19	.00012–.00024/ .003–.006	.069/1.75 (Comp.) .079/2.0 (Upper Oil) 1.58/4.0 (Lower Oil)	.0018–.011/ .045–.27 .0018–.011/ .045–.27 .001–.010/ .025–.255	.008–.014/ .20–.35
1204	2.912–2.913/ 73.992–74.002	2.911–2.912/ 73.955–73.985	.826/21.99				.009–.017/ .25–.45
Simca 5	2.913/74.002						

Piston Ring Assembly

Assemble piston rings in the following sequence: oil pusher ring (lower), oil scraper ring (middle), compression ring (top). Ring gap as measured with a feeler gauge with piston in cylinder should be as follows:

Compression ring (top):
    .009–.017 in. (.25–.45 mm.)
Scraper ring (middle):
    .009–.017 in. (.25–.45 mm.)
Pusher ring (lower):
    .007–.015 (.20–.40 mm.)

Cooling System

Simca 1204

The power unit of the 1204 is cooled by water circulated in a closed and pressurized circuit with a total capacity of 6.9 quarts. Intake manifold and carburetor are heated by hose connection to the cooling circuit. An expansion hose connects the radiator to an expansion bottle which has a pressure-sensitive valve that opens the outlet line when the pressure rises above 8.53 psi, and opens the inlet line when it falls below .56 psi.

The radiator cooling fan is driven by an electric motor, powered by the battery and actuated by a temperature controlled switch and relay.

CAUTION: because the fan is actuated by a temperature-controlled switch, the fan should be disconnected for safety whenever repairs are made on a warm engine. (See ELECTRICAL SYSTEMS, Chapter Five.)

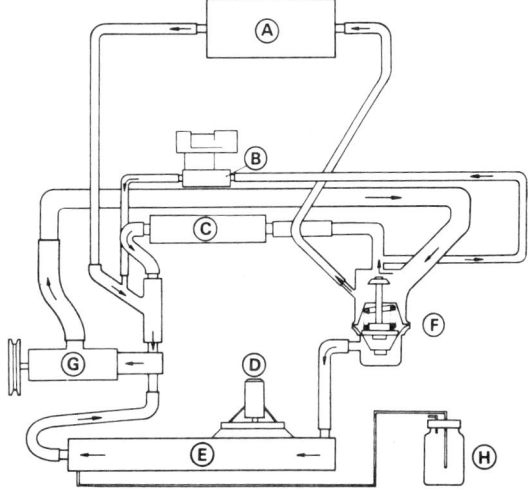

Simca 1204 cooling system:

A Heater-defroster   E Radiator
B Carburetor base   F Thermostat
C Intake manifold   G Water pump
D Radiator cooling fan H Expansion bottle

Radiator Removal

Drain cooling system by removing water pump screw. Remove air cleaner. Disconnect electric fan and remove the assembly. Disconnect water hoses from radiator. Disconnect and remove fan temperature switch and relay. Remove upper radiator bracket and two screws from lower rubber mountings. Tilt radiator toward front and lift up and over engine to remove from car. Install radiator by reverse procedure.

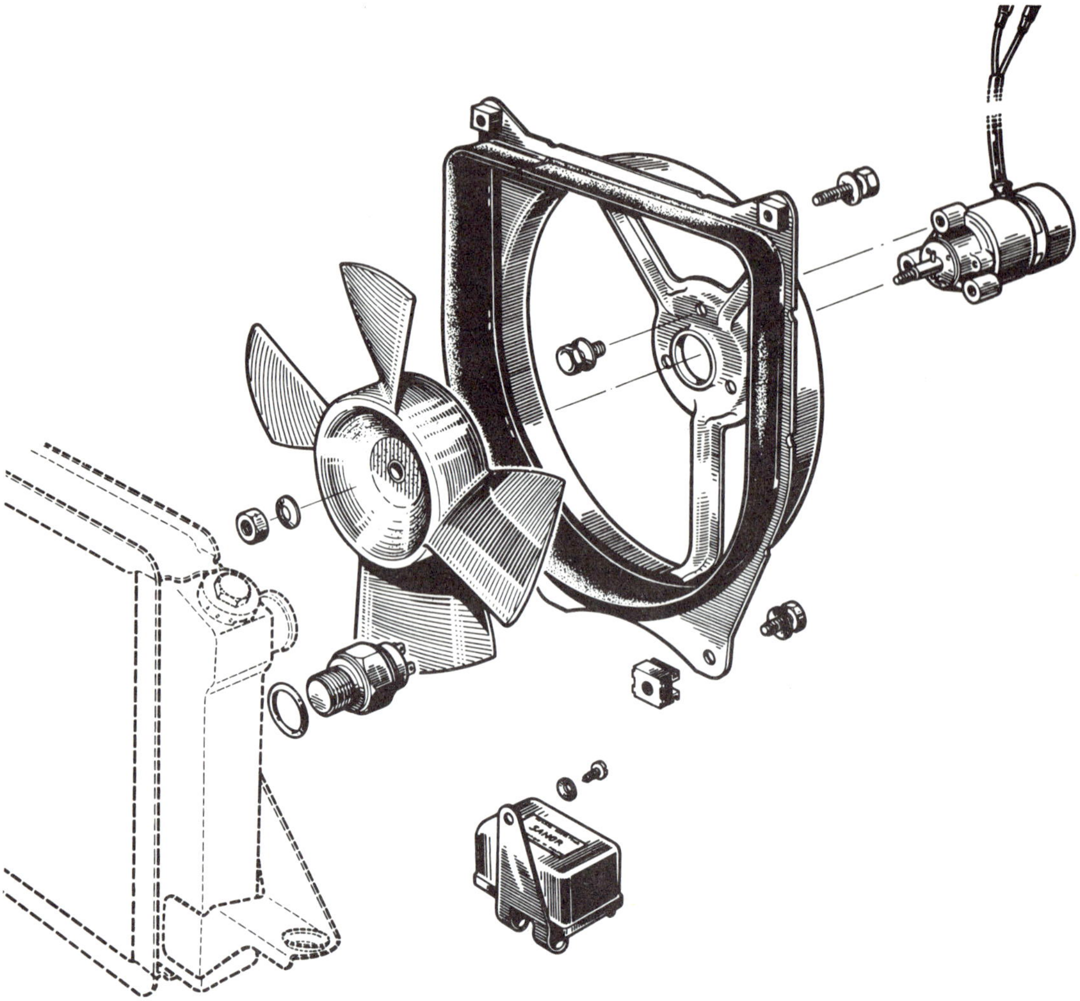

Electric cooling fan components.

Cooling system drain screw.

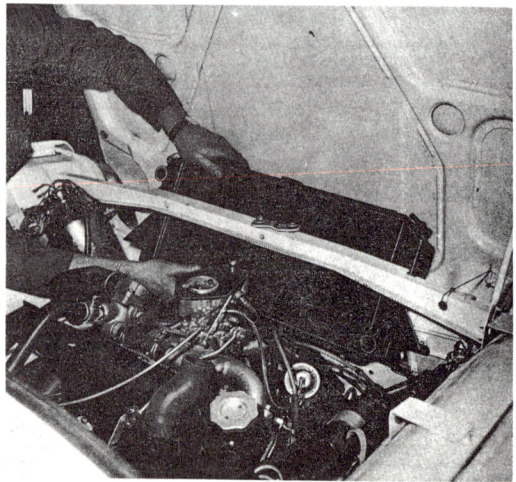

Removing the radiator.

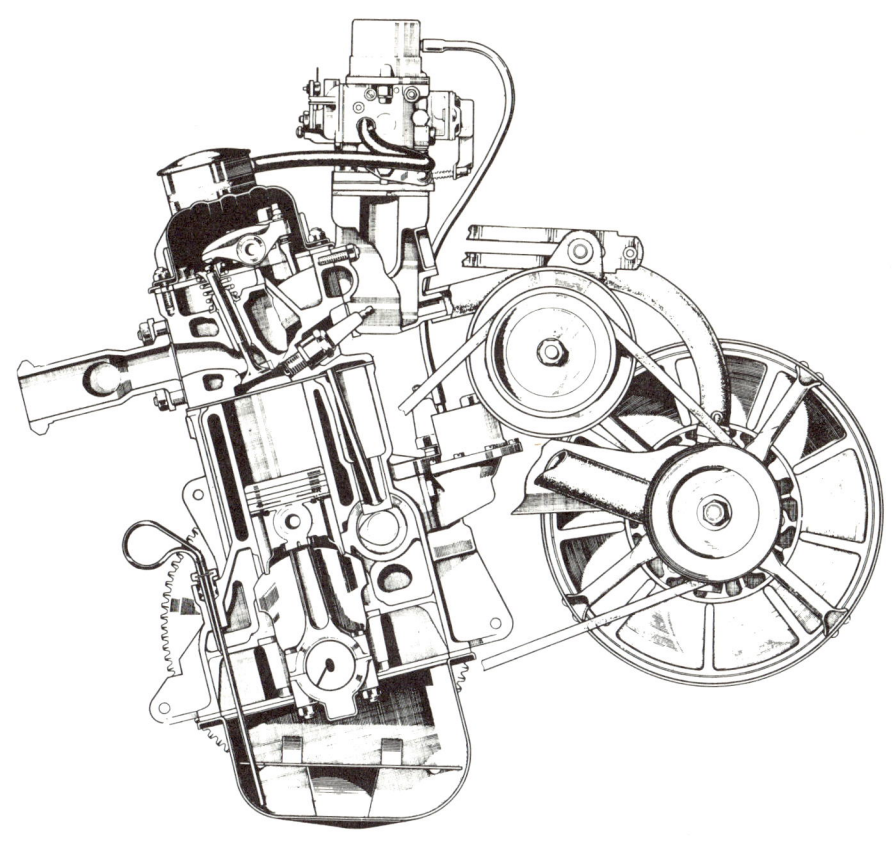

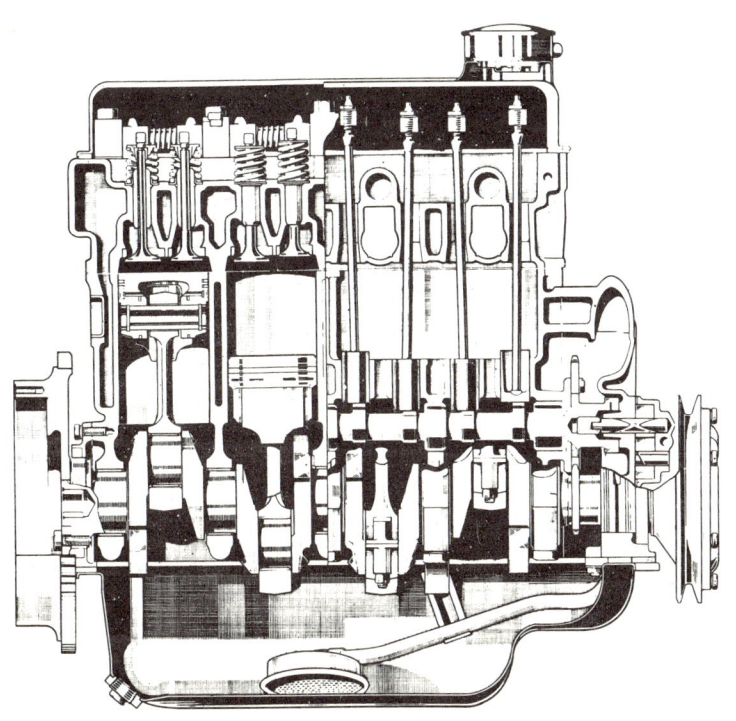

Simca 1000 engine.

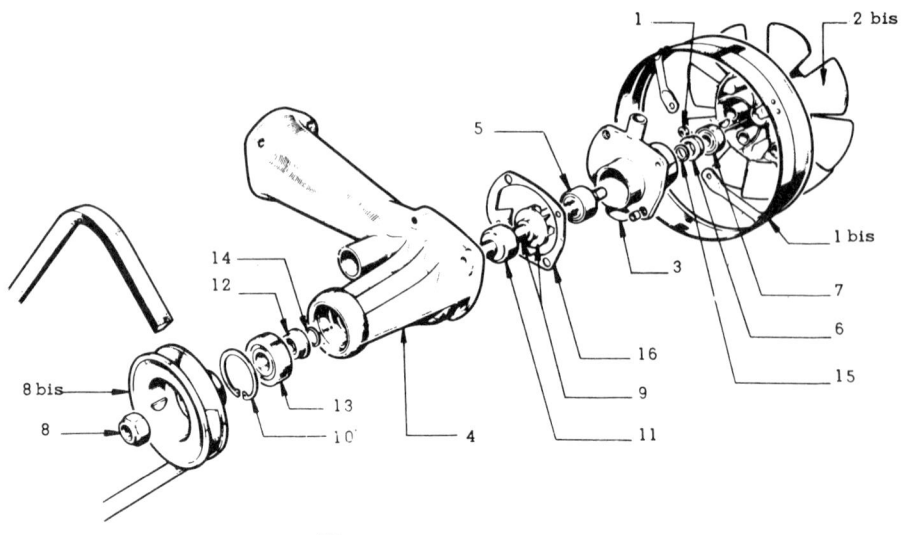

Water pump components.

Engine

Simca 1000

The front of this rear-mounted engine faces the front of the car, and the cylinders are numbered from the front of the engine. Looking at the engine from the rear of the car, the radiator is on the right side, the exhaust manifold on the left, and crankshaft movement is counterclockwise. The engine for the Simca 1000 Coupe has a higher compression ratio and slightly different carburetor settings than the Simca 1000 Sedan.

Water Pump Overhaul

Disassemble water pump by removing two nuts located on each end and removing pulley fan and keys. With a puller, remove cover (3) from main body (4). Remove bearing (7) by inserting a .629 in. (16 mm.) diameter bar inside the graphite seal (5). Remove seal (5) with a .866 in. (22 mm.) diameter bar. Disassemble body (4) by removing shaft (9) with a puller. Remove circlip (10). Remove bearing (13) with the .629 in. diameter bar inserted through inside of seal (11) and remove the seal with the .866 in. bar.

Recondition by lightly sanding shaft and impeller to remove rust. Pitted or corroded parts should be replaced. The seals (5, 11)

and the two nuts at each end should be replaced with new ones when reassembling.

Reassemble water pump by placing bearing (7) and short spacer (6) on cover. Fit bearing (13), circlips (10) and spacer (12) to body. Coat outer sides of seals and housings with sealant and press in seals until they are firmly seated with pump body and cover. Install cover with paper gasket and fit two rings (17) for proper positioning of cover on body. Install fan shroud (1 bis) and tighten screws. Install keys, pulley, and fan, and tighten the two nuts at each end.

Engine Removal

The power plant consisting of the engine and transaxle assembly is supported in the front at one point and in the rear at two points by the rear suspension crossmember. The power plant is removed as a complete unit and lowered from under the raised car onto a cradle which may be made up for use with a hydraulic lift.

Before jacking the car, drain cooling system. Disconnect negative battery cable and wires from ignition coil. Disconnect generator and starter wires and unfasten the bellows between the fan and radiator shrouds. Detach water hoses from cylinder head. Disconnect feed line from fuel pump. Disconnect accelerator control cable and cover. Remove water temperature and oil pressure sensors from engine.

From inside car, remove rear seat. Re-

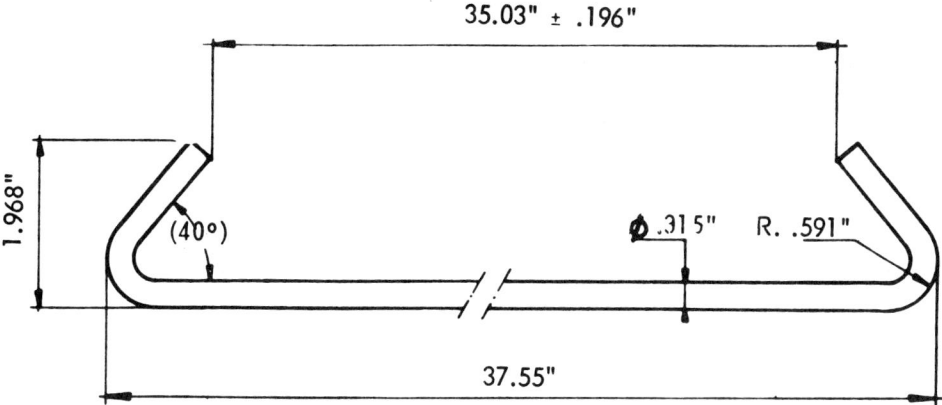

35.03" ± .196"

1.968"

(40°)

φ .315"   R. .591"

37.55"

A rod bent to these dimensions can be used to hold wheel shafts in place in planetary gear.

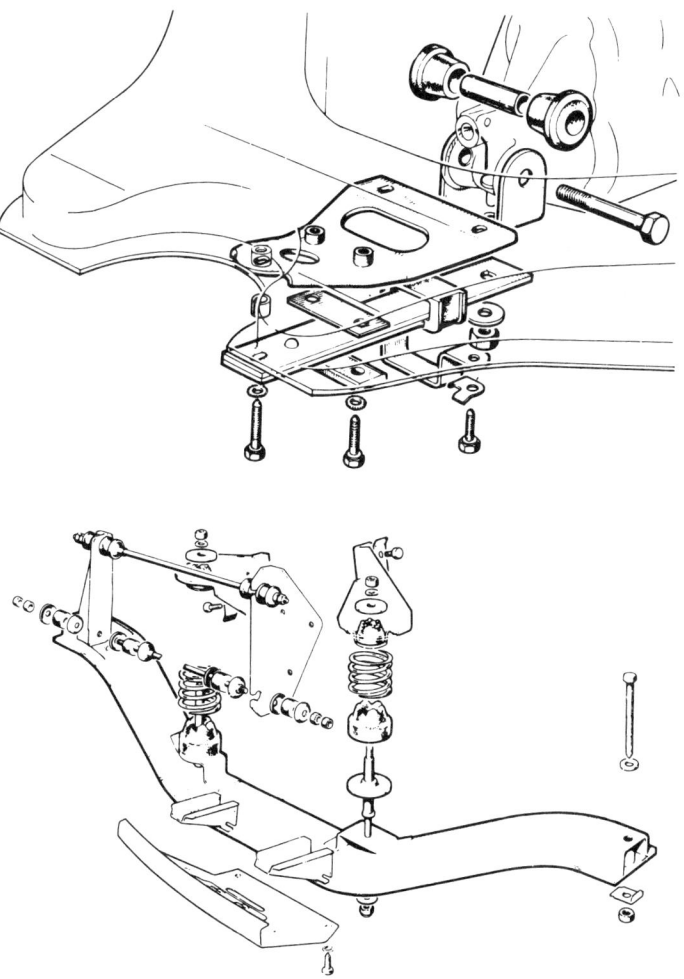

Engine mountings, front (top) and rear (bottom).

move cover from access hole. Disconnect speedometer cable by unscrewing nut and removing key, then disassembling cable stub. Disconnect gearshift control rod.

Hoist car, and from under rear floor remove the protective panel from right side of engine compartment. Disconnect water line between water pump and radiator.

Disconnect drive shafts on the right and left sides where they join the wheel shaft bushings. Remove the rubber thrust bearings from each shaft.

NOTE: a convenient tool for holding each shaft in position in the planetary gear can be made by bending a .315 in. (8 mm.) diameter rod as illustrated.

Lift the power plant slightly to take the strain off the mountings and support it while disassembling the front mounting. Detach the rear support from the right and left side members. Disconnect the hydraulic clutch control. Lower the power plant about six inches being careful not to break the flexible line between the master cylinder and clutch cylinder. Remove clutch cylinder from clutch housing. This should prevent any loss of fluid so that it will not

be necessary to bleed the system at reassembly.

Remove power plant from beneath car. Reinstall the power plant by reversing the above procedure. Two specially designed spring compressors facilitate centering of the rubber bushings for proper positioning of the rear mounting pins. Torque to specifications. Check and adjust clutch fork clearance. Bleed hydraulic system if necessary.

Engine Disassembly

Mark position of flywheel with regard to crankshaft to maintain the same balance when reassembled. Observe numbers and positions of main bearing inserts for proper reassembly. Numbers should face flywheel. Front main bearing inserts have an oil groove in addition to the oil hole in the other inserts. Place the two half washers for the center main bearing with their grooves facing the crankshaft. Check that crankshaft play is between .005 in. (.12 mm.) to .010 in. (.25 mm.). Always use new lockwashers, gaskets and oil seals in reassembling engine.

Pistons and connecting rod bearings are marked for proper reassembly. Replace pistons, if necessary, with four pistons of the same type. Place the pistons with their front marks toward the timing gears. Warm piston to 176°F (80°C), fit wrist pin and insert snap rings. Install rings with top mark facing piston upper end up, and end-gaps evenly spaced around the piston. Assemble connecting rod and bearing with the marks toward the camshaft. Tighten connecting rod nuts to 17 ft. lbs. (2.3 kgm.).

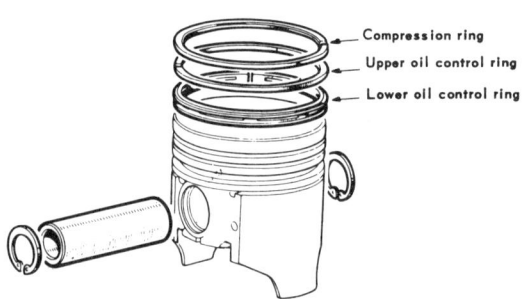

Compression ring
Upper oil control ring
Lower oil control ring

Piston ring and wrist pin installation.

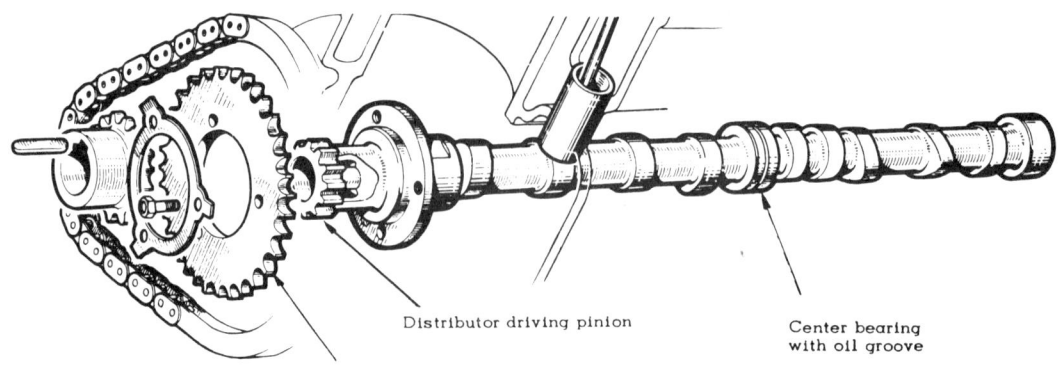

Distributor driving pinion

Center bearing with oil groove

Camshaft driving gear

Timing gear installation.

Place piston No. 1 in top dead center position.

Place timing gear key on crankshaft and fit camshaft after oiling bearing. Check camshaft play by assembling cover with a plastic gauge between the bearing face and camshaft. Resultant thickness of gauge should not be less than .016 in. (.4 mm.). Install timing gears and chain with marks facing each other. Secure camshaft gear by holding it in position while turning crankshaft until three mounting holes line up with gear holes (Holes line up in one position only). Tighten screws to 7 ft. lbs. (1 kgm.). Install thrust washer on crankshaft end with ground face out. Install timing gear cover with new gasket and seal. Install inner seal against crankshaft washer (do not turn), install spring and second seal with one notch facing a centering dog. This cup will be temporarily held in position by the oil separator hub seal. Install oil pump driving gear and oil pump after coating mating surfaces of pump and cover with oil. Torque pump and make sure it rotates freely. Install oil separator hub on shaft. Timing marks should face each other with piston No. 1 in TDC position. Install diffusion cone, oil separator cover, and tighten timing gear cover screws. Secure oil sump line and install oil pressure sensor being careful not to damage cylinder block by excessive tightening. Proper torque is 20 ft. lbs. (2.7 kgm.). Install valves with a spring compressor after lubricating stems. Bore the guides if worn or scratched and use oversize stems.

Install cylinder head gasket using guide studs placed in the cylinder head at the front and rear on the exhaust manifold side to center the oversize gasket holes with the cylinder head mounting holes.

Assemble rocker shafts, brackets and springs, insert valve pushrods, place assembly on cylinder head, and center rocker arms with valve stems. Rotate engine to free each bracket from valve spring tension. Torque cylinder head bolts to 45 ft. lbs. (6.2 kgm.) in the proper sequence. Adjust rocker clearance to .012 in. (.30 mm.) for intake valves and .014 in. (.35 mm.) for exhaust valves. Install rocker cover and gasket.

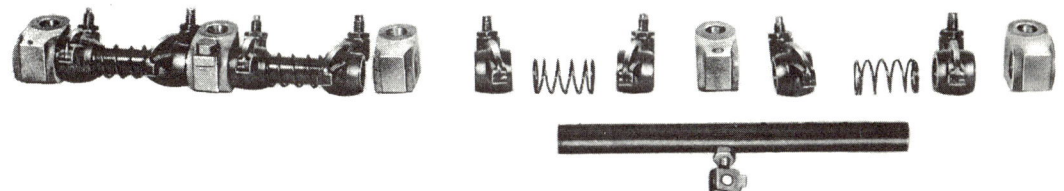

Rocker arm and shaft assembly.

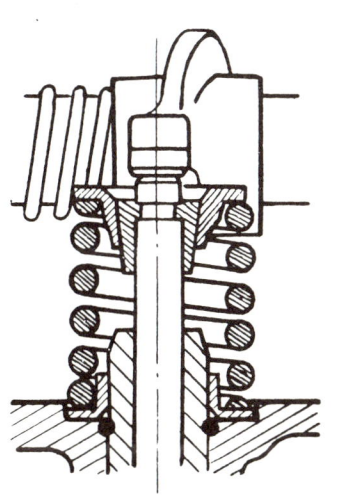

Proper fitting

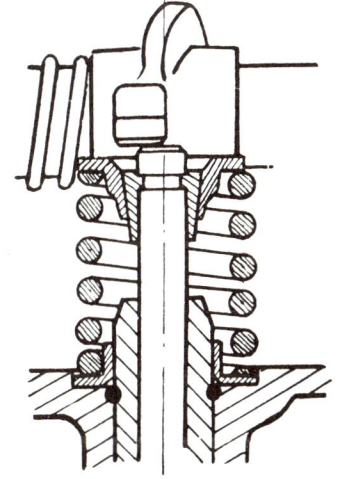

Wrong fitting

Proper centering of rocker arm and valve stem.

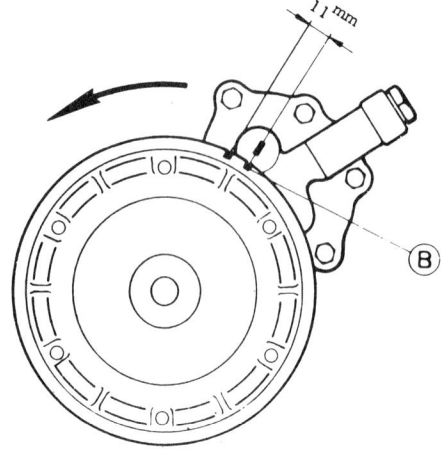

Set distributor timing so that points open when oil separator mark A (see illustration) is opposite oil pump mark, and mark B of oil separator and oil pump cover face each other with piston No. 1 on TDC position. Rotation is counterclockwise. With crankshaft in this position, check that cylinder No. 4 rocker arms are lifted, cylinder No. 1 being on compression stroke. Place distributor rotor to fire No. 1 cylinder plug wire.

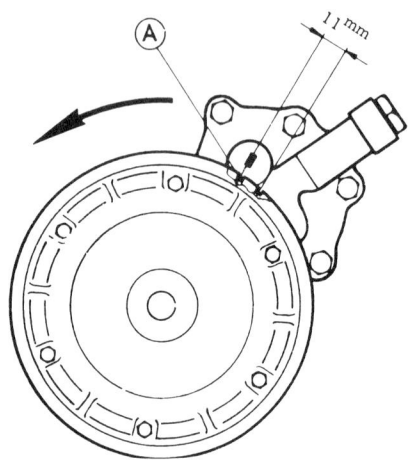

Cylinder head tightening sequence.

When mark B faces oil pump mark (top), piston No. 1 should be in TDC position. Set distributor so that points open when mark A faces oil pump mark (bottom). Engine turns counterclockwise.

Simca Carburetors

The Solex downdraft carburetors on Simca cars differ mainly in jet sizes and adjustments. Carburetors on the later Simcas include a dual venturi choke tube and oil breather connection. Familiarity with carburetor principles is helpful when overhauling the carburetors.

Float Circuit

The float mechanism is a conventional circuit that maintains a constant fuel level so that fuel atomization at all jets will be uniform under different vacuum conditions.

Operation of the float circuit is simple. As the float drops, a needle valve is released that admits fuel from the pump. The rising fuel level lifts the float to its former level, reclosing the valve. The assembly is

Solex Carburetor Specifications

Car Model	Carburetor Type	Venturi	Main Jet	Correction Jet	Idle Jet	Idling Air Bleed	Emulsion Tube	Pump Injector	Pump Jet	Econo-Stat	Fuel Jet	Float Valve In./MM.	Float Weight Ozs./GR.	Air Jet In./MM.
1000 (To #5043943)	32 PBIC	21	100	180	40	120	17	52	40	85	115	.06/1.5	.29/5.7	.178/4.5
1000 (From #5043944)	32 PBIC	23	100	180	40	120	17	52	40	85	125	.06/1.5	.29/5.7	.178/4.5
1000 (From #5200021)	32 PBIC	25	112	210	45	100	28	50	40	100	125	.06/1.5	.29/5.7	.178/4.5
1000 (From #5310830)	32 PBIC	25	110	210	40	130	71	50	40	55	125	.06/1.5	.29/5.7	.178/4.5
1204	32 BISA													
Simca 5	32 PBICT	24	112	165	45	100	10		50	65			.29/5.7	

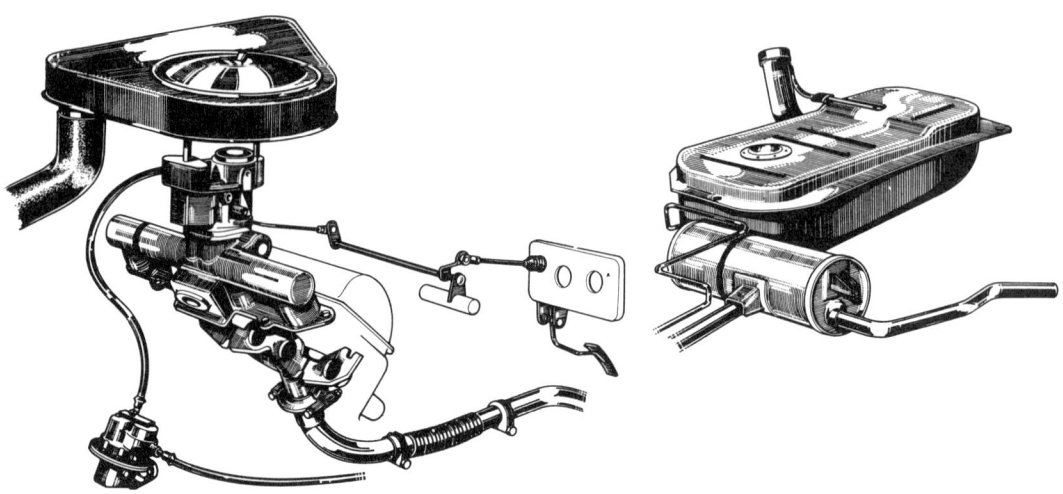

Simca 1204 fuel and exhaust system.

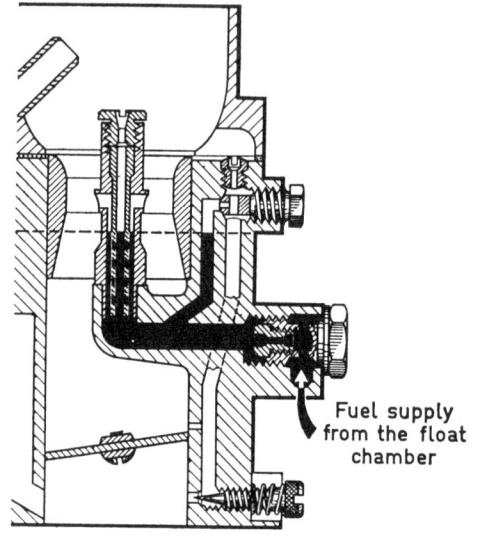

Fuel supply
from the float
chamber

The float mechanism keeps a constant fuel level for uniform atomization.

designed for a fuel pumping pressure of approximately 2 psi. Higher pump pressures are compensated for by substituting smaller needle valves. Needle valve assemblies wear quickly and so should be replaced with each carburetor overhaul.

Starting Circuit

A choke starting circuit provides rich fuel-air mixture to the cylinders of a cold engine for easy starting and smooth warm up. In the Solex 32PB1C starting circuit, fuel from the float chamber mixes with air after passing through a cable-operated disc-type valve. The mixture is drawn into the manifold either through a separate throat or through the main barrel below the throttle butterfly plate.

Idling Circuit

The idling system uses a mixture-volume control screw (idle speed adjustment) located below the throttle valve (also called butterfly or plate). Fuel for idling is usually taken after passing through the main jet (mono-jet idling) and is cut off when the main jet begins to function. At increased engine speeds, the fuel, once flowing to the idling system, is siphoned away from the idling ducts and passes through the complete main jet system instead.

Progression (second idle) Circuit

As the throttle butterfly is opened, vacuum at the idle adjustment orifice is lessened because more air passes around the butterfly. With lower vacuum, less mixture is drawn into the throat at the moment when more air is passing into the manifold. To provide more fuel, one or more orifices are drilled into the carburetor at precise points in line with the butterfly. These holes, comprising the progression circuit (second idle), ensure a smooth transfer of fuel mixture from idling to the main jet circuit. The progression circuit eliminates flat-spots or pauses when the main jet begins to function. The progression circuit is easily

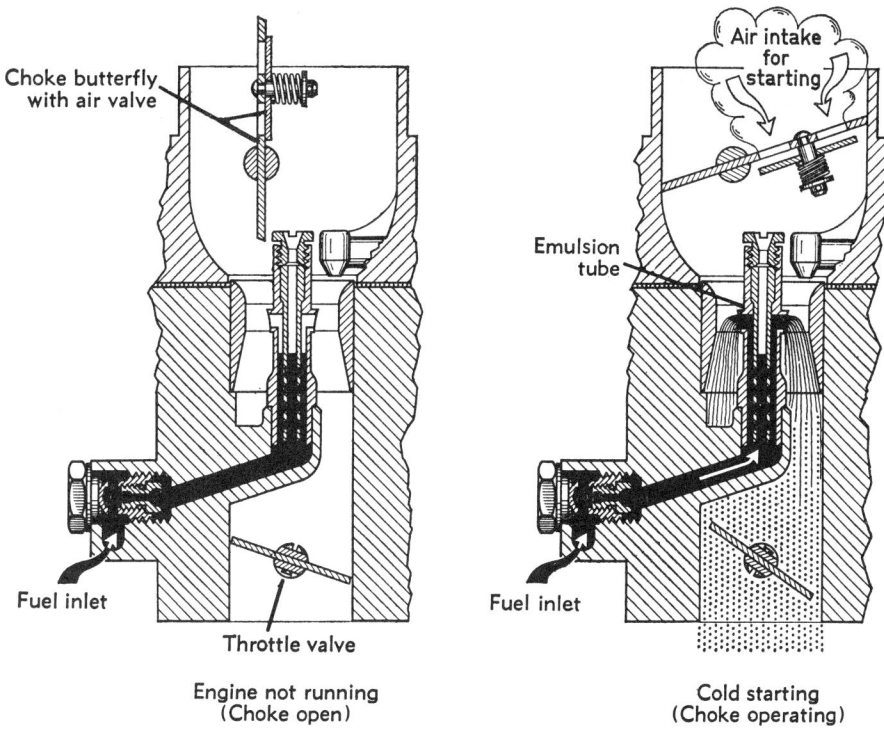

Choke system using air valve on choke butterfly.

clogged if sediment enters the carburetor. Also, dislocation of the throttle valve due to abuse of the linkage critically changes the relationship of the valve to the orifice.

In general, if the orifice is above the throttle plate at the point where additional fuel (second idle) is needed, a flat spot occurs in acceleration. If the reverse is true —the hole is below the plate when fuel is needed—a rich mixture occurs that cannot be adjusted out.

An easy test to check the progression circuit (after overhauling and adjusting the carburetor) is to turn the throttle stop screw to the point just before the main jet starts to operate (approx. 800 rpm). Then, slowly back out the idle mixture screw. If the engine speeds up, the progression is too lean. When turning the idle screw in, if the engine speeds up, the progression feed is too rich.

Main Jet Circuit

The main jet circuit, consisting of the venturi (choke tube), main jet, high speed air bleed (air correction jet) and main vent (emulsion) tube, supplies fuel-air mixture for normal engine speeds. Different carburetors have various arrangements of the main jet assemblies. The differences are most often in the way the air is supplied and in the layout of the adjustable parts.

Acceleration Circuit

The longer the induction manifold, the greater the need for acceleration pumps to quickly inject emulsified (mixed with air) fuel into the carburetor throat as the throttle butterfly is suddenly opened.

As the pump plunger moves upward, fuel is drawn into the plunger chamber through the strainer and inlet check valve. When the throttle plate is opened, the accelerator plunger is pushed downward, discharging fuel through the accelerator jet into the venturi. The size of the accelerator jet determines the duration of the fuel injection. Both the amount of fuel injected and the duration of the injection are adjustable. Fuel quantity is changed by adjusting the length of the control rod. Duration of injection depends on the size of the accelerator jet and compression of the pump spring.

Solex makes three basic types of acceleration pumps. Neutral pumps with identification numbers ending in 2 (e.g. 72, 82, or 92) are for carburetors feeding normal four-cylinder engines. Rich pumps with identifications ending in 3 (e.g. 73, 83, or 93) are suited for carburetors feeding four-cylinder sports models, six-cylinder normal engines, and super-charged engines. Pumps with a final number 4 (weak pumps) are designed for carburetors directly supplying only one, two, or three cylinders.

Power Circuit (High Speed Enrichment)

High-speed enrichment devices are designed to enrich the fuel-air mixture automatically in high speed ranges when great volumes of air are being drawn into the engine.

Solex has the enrichment device connected with the main jet circuit. As vacuum increases, additional fuel-air mixture is pulled from the enrichment circuit through a cross channel into the main circuit. The amount added increases progressively with engine speed.

Altitude Corrector

Thinner air at high altitudes, 3200–4900 (1000–1500 M), causes the fuel-air mixture to be richer. Solex among others has available an altitude corrector that is fitted in place of the main jet carrier. It progressively reduces the flow of fuel into the main jet as atmospheric pressure decreases in higher altitudes. In substantially different altitudes, the main jet size must be different. To compensate for higher altitudes, the main jet is approximately 6 percent smaller for every 3,000 feet.

Carburetor Operation

Idle speed air required for the enricher, for the main jet mixture, and for ventilating the float bowl is drawn from the main air intake of the carburetor and thus through the air filter.

The manually operated enricher assures proper starting and driving carburetion during cold weather operation. It is used only until the engine has reached its normal operating temperature. Richness of mixture is varied by use of the control cable on

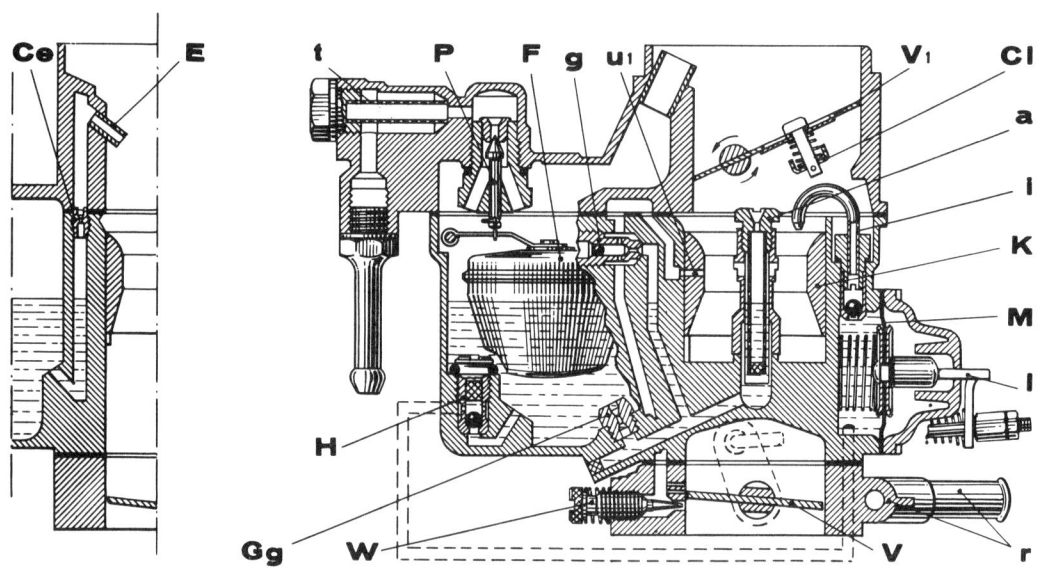

Solex Type 32 BISA carburetor with Econostat (left) for high speed fuel injection:

VI	Choke butterfly		a	Correction metering jet
Cl	Choke air valve		V	Throttle
g	Idling jet		M	Diaphragm of accelerator pump
W	Volume (richness) control screw		l	Pump lever
ul	Emulsion air orifice		i	Calibrated injector
K	Venturi		E	Fuel injector tube
Gg	Main jet		H	Ball check valve

the dash, full richness being obtained when the control cable is pulled all the way out. During warm-up period, the control cable is pushed back half way.

Feeding of engine at idle speed is controlled by the jet (g). Richness of idle-speed mixture is adjusted by the volume screw (W), allowing a very precise adjustment of engine. Air intake is through a calibrated orifice located in the body of the carburetor in a recessed space beneath the venturi (K).

Fuel air mixture for driving speed is supplied by the main jet (Gg) and by venturi (K). The correct balance is automatically obtained by air passing through and being calibrated by the metering jet (a). The emulsion tube is located underneath the air metering jet. The calibration of this part should not be changed. It should be removed and cleaned at every carburetor overhaul.

The pump injects a certain amount of supplementary fuel at the time of acceleration. In idling position, the throttle (V) is closed, and the diaphragm (M), held in position by a spring, allows a supply of fuel to build up. When the throttle is opened by the accelerator linkage, the lever (I) presses on the diaphragm, forcing fuel from the supply through the pump jet (i) into the nozzle and then into the venturi. The dimension of the pump jet controls the rate of discharge. The ball check (H) has a screen which should be cleaned when cleaning the carburetor.

Carburetor Overhaul

Carburetor part replacement kits are recommended for each overhaul. Kits contain a complete set of gaskets and new parts to replace those that deteriorate most rapidly. It is advisable to use all of the new parts supplied in the kits.

The Solex carburetor can be removed easily after air filter, control linkage, fuel lines, vacuum advance and water hoses have been disconnected. Note position of air filter on carburetor for correct replacement. Remove mounting capscrews and carburetor from engine.

Disassemble carburetor as follows with reference to exploded view drawings. Keep look-alike parts separated to prevent accidental interchange at assembly. Note all jet sizes.

1. Remove float chamber cover by removing three screws.
2. Remove float from cover by releasing needle valve lock clip and sliding float arm off pivot pin.
3. Remove needle valve assembly from cover.
4. Remove pump injector tube with a screwdriver.
5. Remove correction jet and emulsion tube.
6. Remove enricher jet.
7. Remove pilot jet.
8. Remove main jet carrier and jet.
9. Remove pump jet.
10. Remove pump ball check valve (check for stuck ball).
11. Remove enricher air jet.
12. Remove volume control screw.
13. Remove choke control cover.

NOTE: choke lever has identifying number 3.

14. Remove accelerator pump housing with a screwdriver.
15. To replace butterfly valve and shaft, remove nut from shaft, remove butterfly set screws and butterfly valve, then remove shaft.

Cleaning and inspecting carburetor parts. Wash carburetor parts—except diaphragm—in solvent, and blow dry with compressed air. Carburetors have numerous small passages that can be fouled by carbon and gummy deposits. Soak metal parts in carburetor solvent until thoroughly clean. However, the solvent will weaken or destroy cork, plastic, and leather components, so these parts should be wiped with a clean, lint-free cloth instead. Remember, breath carries moisture which induces oxidation. Clean diaphragms only in mild soap solution to prevent deterioration. Clean jets and valves separately to avoid interchanging them during reassembly.

Check the shaft of the throttle valve for too much play that allows air leakage (affecting starting and idling). Inspect float spindle and other moving parts for wear. Replace if worn. Replace float if gasoline has leaked into it. The accelerator pump check valves (no-return ball valve) should pass air one way but not the other. Test for proper valve seating by blowing and sucking on valve and replace if necessary.

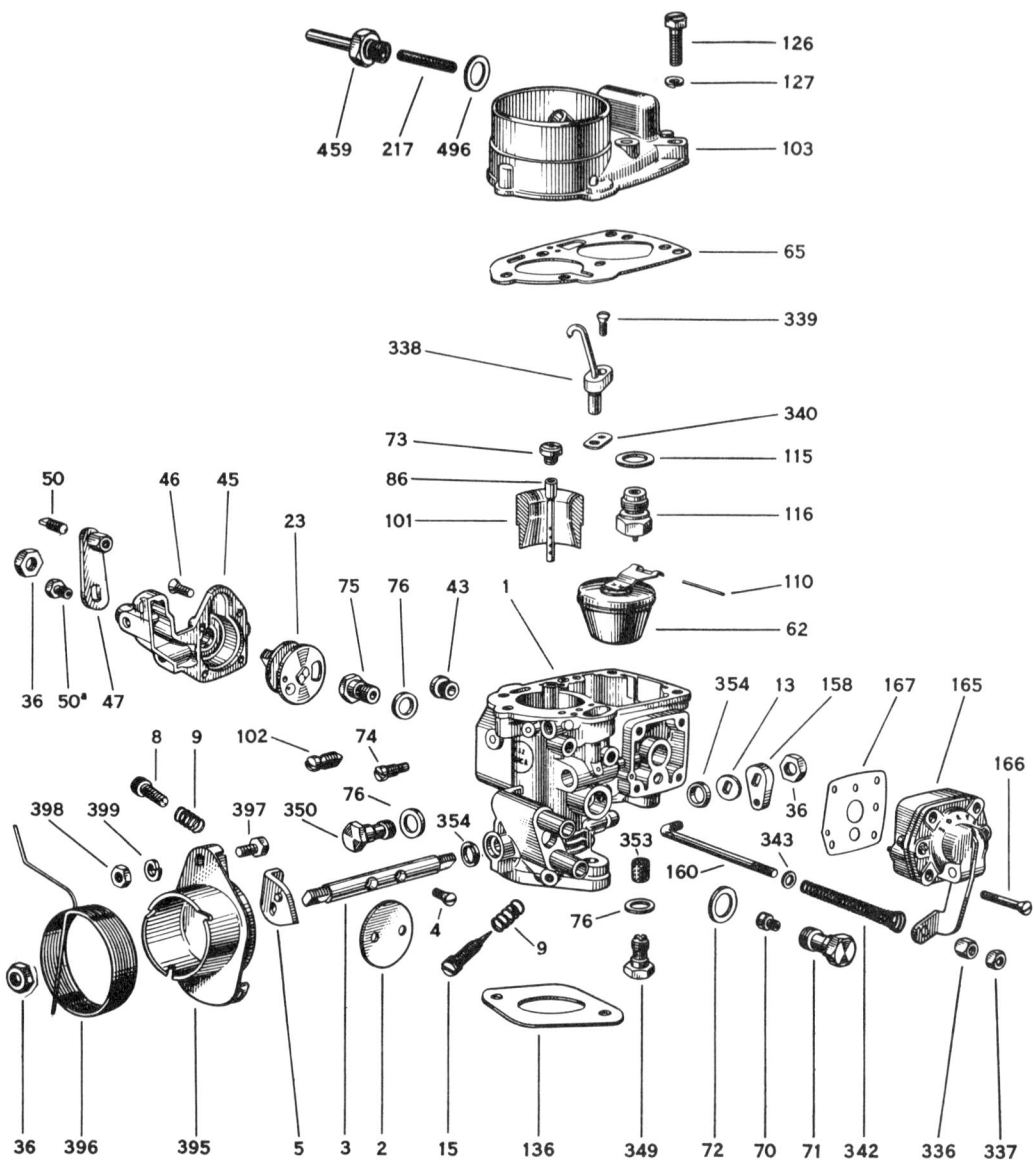

Exploded view of Solex PBICA carburetor.

Wash it again to remove breath moisture. Carefully clean all fuel channels in the float bowl and cover. Blow out these channels in both directions so that ball valves and seats are clean and action is free.

Replace the accelerator pump diaphragm because it loses properties when exposed to air. Replace the carburetor flange gasket. While the carburetor is disassembled, check the bowl cover with a straight edge for warped surfaces.

Do not tighten needle valves into seats. Uneven jetting will result. Inspect valves and seats for wear and damage. Replace if necessary.

Reassemble carburetor in reverse order of disassembly referring to drawings. Use new gasketing and other soft parts where needed.

Reassemble accelerator pump by placing spring in pump body lower section, then diaphragm assembly in pump cover and fastening both groups together with short center pump-cover screws. Hold pump arm steady while tightening screws to keep diaphragm from distorting. In assembling

1. BODY with throttle spindle, butterfly, screws and dust proof rings
2. Throttle butterfly
3. Throttle spindle
4. Throttle butterfly, fixing screw
5. Throttle spindle abutment plate only
8. Slow running adjustment screw
9. Slow running adjustment screw spring
13. Throttle spindle washer (for throttle butterfly)
15. Volume control screw
9. Volume control screw spring
23. Starter valve complete
36. Starter spindle end nut
36. Throttle spindle end nut
43. Starter air jet (Ga)
45. Starter cover
46. Starter cover fixing screw
47. Starter lever with cable swivel
50. Starter cable swivel screw
50a. Starter cable locking screw
62. Float (F)
65. Float chamber gasket
70. Main jet (Gg)
71. Main jet carrier
72. Main jet carrier washer

73. Correction jet (a)
74. Pilot jet (gN)
75. Starter petrol jet (Gs)
76. Gp, Gs and pump inlet valve washer
86. Emulsion tube (s)
101. Choke tube (K)
102. Choke tube fixing screw
103. FLOAT CHAMBER COVER with petrol union
110. Float toggle spindle
115. Needle valve washer
116. Needle valve complete with washer (P)
126. Float chamber assembly screw
127. Spring washer for same
136. Flange washer
158. Pump intermediate actuating lever
160. Pump control rod
165. ACCELERATING PUMP
166. Pump assembly fixing screw
167. Pump body gasket
217. Filter gauze
336. Pump control rod adjustment nut
337. Adjustment nut counternut
338. Pump injector assembly
339. Pump injector support fixing screw

340. Pump injector support gasket
342. Pump control rod spring
343. Control rod retaining washer
349. Pump inlet valve
350. Pump jet (Gp)
353. Pump filter gauze
354. Dust proof ring
395. Throttle control
396. Throttle control return spring
397. Cable fixing screw for throttle control
398. Nut for cable fixing screw
399. Spring washer for cable fixing screw
459. Petrol union
496. Washer for petrol union

CURRENT CARBURETOR SETTING

Choke tube	K = 25
Main jet	Gg = 130
Air correction jet	a = 170
Pilot jet	g = 50
Emulsion tube	s = 19
Needle valve	1.7 mm
Float	5.7 gr.

ACCELERATING PUMP NO. 72

Pump jet	Gp = 45
Starter air jet	Ga = 6.5
Starter fuel jet	Gs = 110

carburetor parts, tighten all screws gradually and alternately.

Install the carburetor after installing the diffuser, with the small inside diameter in the cylinder head. Use new gasket and reconnect linkage, fuel lines, and hoses.

Float Level Adjustment

With the engine idling, the fuel pump delivering gas at the specified pressure, and the car sitting perfectly level, the needle valve on the carburetor should be partially closed. When the engine is shut off, the needle valve should close completely.

Float level is adjusted by installing a thicker or thinner gasket under the needle valve. Thin gaskets raise the fuel level; thick gaskets lower it. Further adjustment is possible by bending the float arm.

Idle Adjustment

The engine must be warm, and the spark plugs and points in good condition.

With the engine idling:

1. Slightly tighten throttle stop screw (Z) to increase the speed of the engine.

2. Loosen volume control screw (W) until engine begins to idle roughly. Then tighten screw slowly until engine idles smoothly.

3. Slowly loosen stop screw (Z) to adjust engine idle to approximately 620 rpm.

NOTE: never completely tighten the volume screw (W).

Fuel Pump Removal

The fuel pump is removed by disconnecting the two fuel lines, and removing the front and rear screws, two gaskets and a fiber shim. On early cars, the oil breather pipe must also be disconnected.

CAUTION: when reinstalling the pump, do not use screws that are any longer than the original mounting screws. Longer screws may reach and block the camshaft.

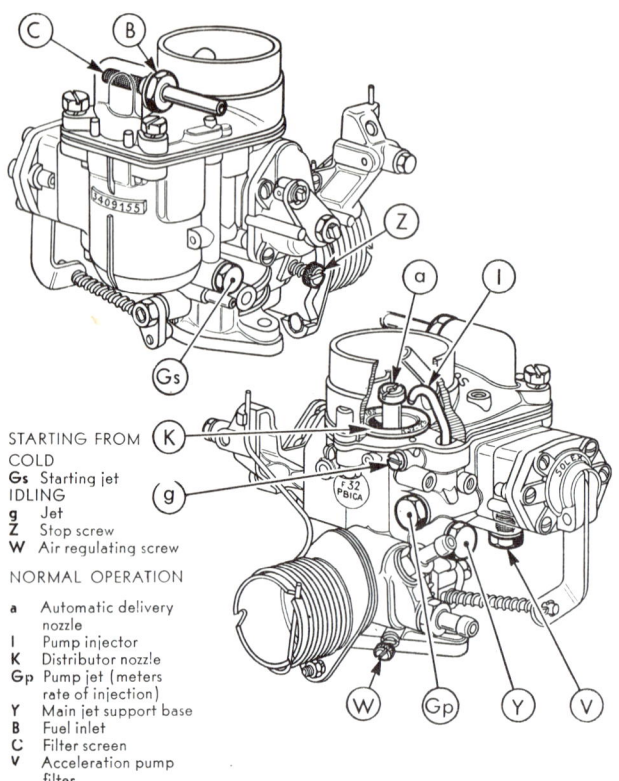

STARTING FROM
COLD
Gs Starting jet
IDLING
g Jet
Z Stop screw
W Air regulating screw

NORMAL OPERATION

a Automatic delivery
       nozzle
I Pump injector
K Distributor nozzle
Gp Pump jet (meters
        rate of injection)
Y Main jet support base
B Fuel inlet
C Filter screen
V Acceleration pump
       filter

Solex carburetor parts and adjustments.

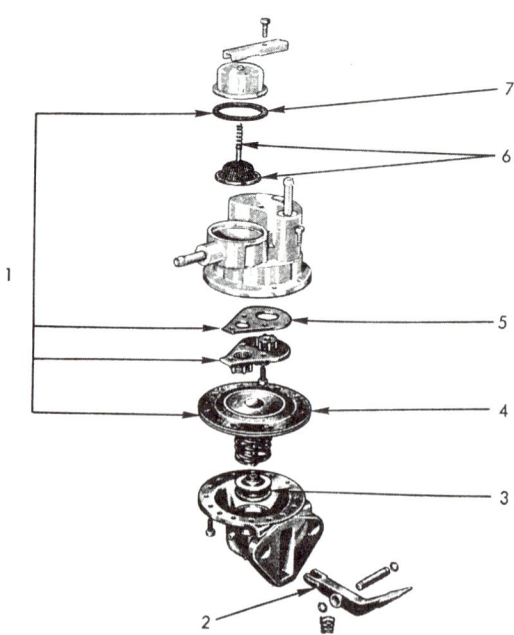

Type SEV fuel pump components:

1 Pump repair package   5 Gasket
2 Arm   6 Screen and spring
3 Spring guide   7 Gasket
4 Diaphragm

Engine Electrical Components

The Simca 1000 employs a Ducellier ignition system and Paris-Rhone starter, generator and regulator. The Simca 1204 uses a Paris-Rhone or Ducellier starter, a Ducellier or SEV ignition system and an alternator rather than the d.c. generator. The 1204 also uses an electric-motor-driven fan rather than the conventional engine-driven fan for radiator cooling. All cars of both series are equipped with 12-volt, negative ground electrical systems.

Starter Overhaul

Remove starter after first disconnecting ungrounded side of battery and then starter wiring. Check condition of bushings and replace if necessary. Bushings are self lubricating, eliminating any need for atten-

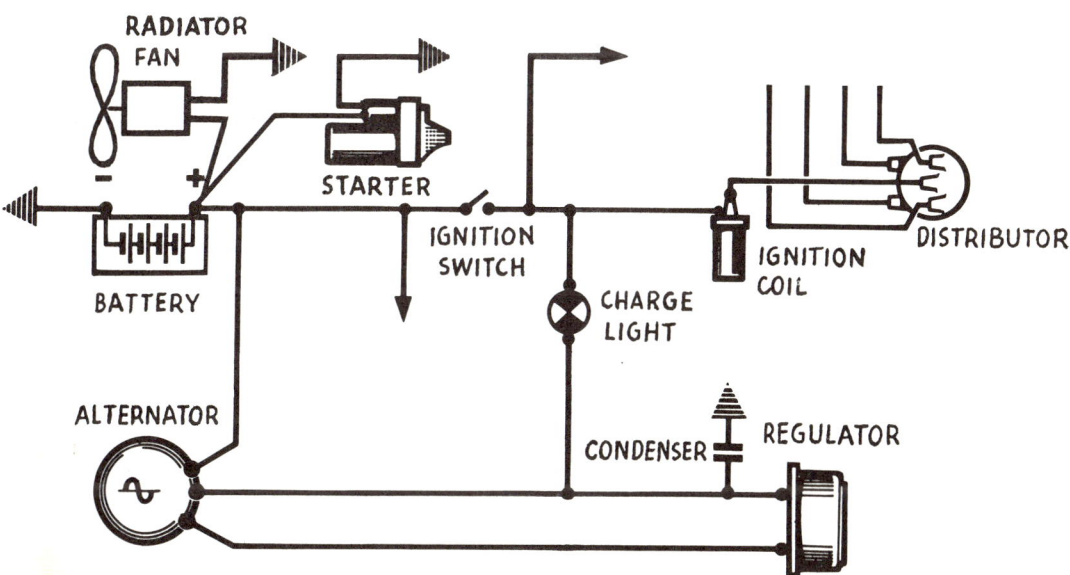

Simca 1204 engine electrical components.

Electrical Equipment Specifications

Car Model	BATTERY		GENERATOR				Alternator Output Watts	REGULATOR		STARTER		Brush Tension Ozs./Grs.
	Cap. Amp.-Hrs.	Volts Ground	Make	Ident. No.	Output Watts	Brush Tension Ozs./Grs.		Make	Ident. No.	Make	Ident. No.	
1000	40	12 Neg.	Paris-Rhone	G10R34	350	15.7–17.5/ 450–500		Paris-Rhone	YTD21	Paris-Rhone		16/ 450
1204	55	12 Neg.					330			Paris-Rhone/ Ducellier		
Simca 5		12 Neg.	Paris-Rhone	R10R16						Ducellier	D8E14	16/ 450
1118	55	12 Neg.					25(Amp)					

tion in service. Check condition of brushes, for free movement in brush holders, and for proper tension of 16 ozs. Brushes should be replaced if length is less than .32 in. (8 mm.). Check commutator for scratches or wear. Maximum out-of-round tolerance for this part is .002 in. (.05 mm.). Undercut mica if necessary between commutator bars. Lubricate drive pinion splines before reassembly.

Adjust Paris-Rhone starter clearance between front stop and drive pinion in actuated position as follows:

1. Operate solenoid with reduced voltage (10 v) by energizing the two small terminals. The drive then comes up to actuated position, but does not rotate.

2. Push armature and drive backward to take up clearance.

3. Make sure clearance between pinion and front stop is .04–.08 in. (1–2 mm.).

4. Adjust if required by adjusting yoke controlling fork after depressing backing cup for return spring of plunger.

NOTE: solenoid should not remain energized for more than a few seconds to avoid damage to windings.

Adjust Ducellier starter drive mechanism so that backward movement of pinion is 2.62 in. (65.5 mm.). Then add or remove washers behind spacer to make pinion travel 3.28 in. (82 mm.). Screw stop nut in or out, and install pin. Take up excess longitudinal play in solenoid drive by the following adjustments in the unactuated position.

Remove plug, and completely loosen adjusting nut. Then tighten adjusting nut until play of drive disappears.

Unscrew adjusting nut one-quarter turn and reinstall plug.

Distributor Adjustment

For Ducellier or SEV distributors, check breaker points for a clearance of .019 in. (.48 mm.) and contact pressure of about 21 ozs. (600 grs.). Cam or dwell angle should be 55–57° with an initial setting of 6° of advance on the crankshaft for the 1204; 8° for the 1000 up to 1963; and 12° for the 1000 starting with 1963.

Charging Equipment

Simca 1204

Battery charging equipment for the 1204 consists of an alternator and regulator. The alternator, which is an alternating current generator, contains two rectifier diodes that change the alternating current to direct current for supply to the battery. A third diode is in series with the charge warning light. The one-way action of this diode prevents the battery from discharging through the warning light when the ignition switch is off.

Regulator Operation

The regulator is a vibrating relay inserted in the alternator excitation circuit, and its function is to control the output of the alternator. One of its two terminals (EXC) is connected to the alternator excitation terminal and the other (+ or BAT) is connected to the positive terminal of the

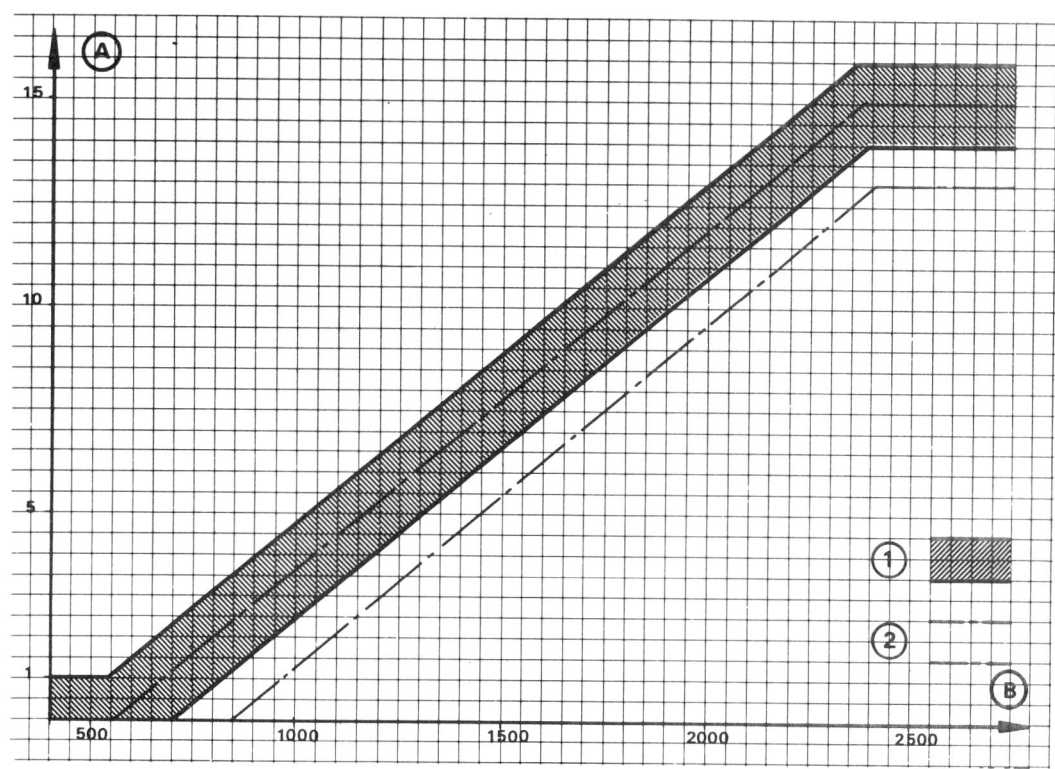

Centrifugal advance of 1204 distributor in degrees (A) at distributor RPM (B).

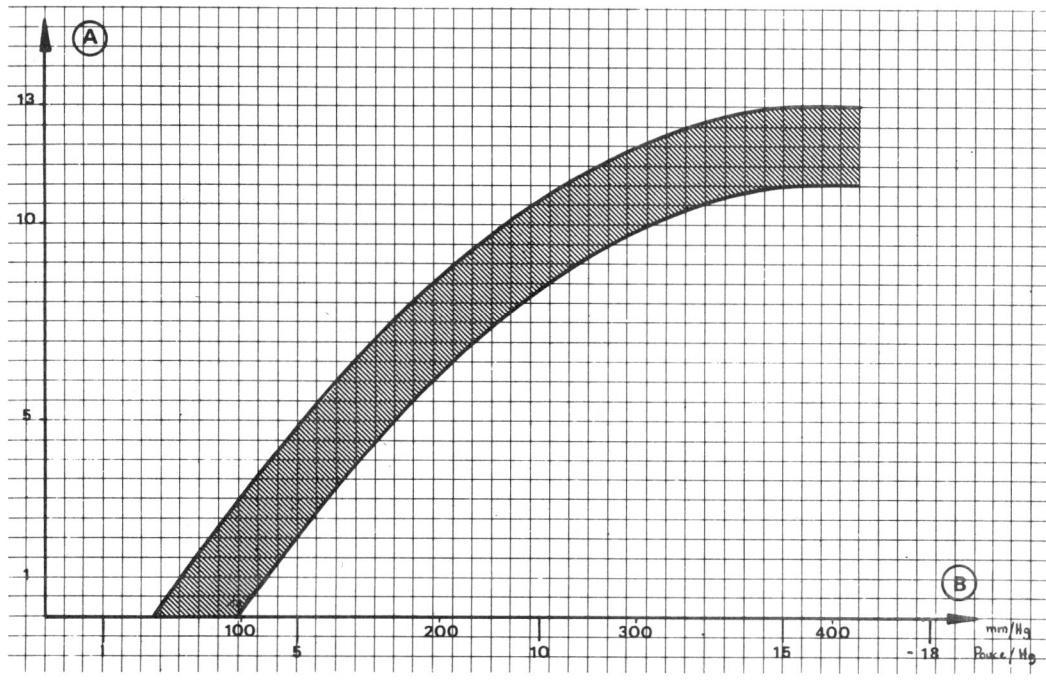

Vacuum advance of 1204 distributor in degrees (A) at distributor rpm (B).

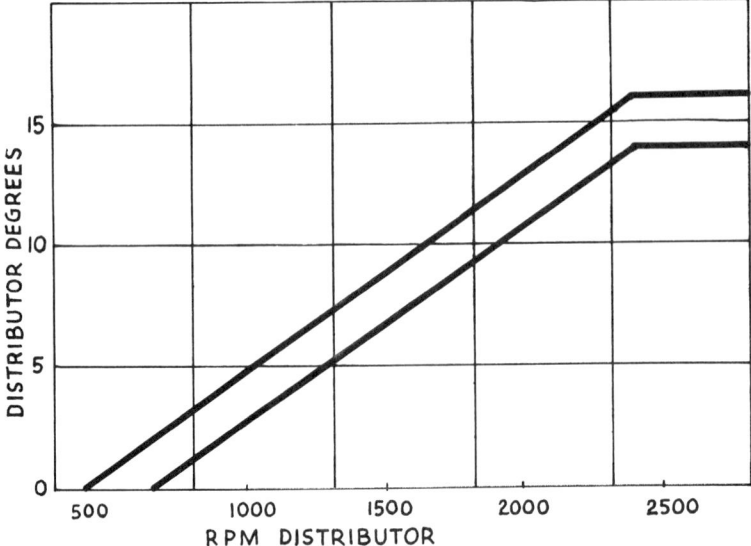

Centrifugal advance of 1000 distributor.

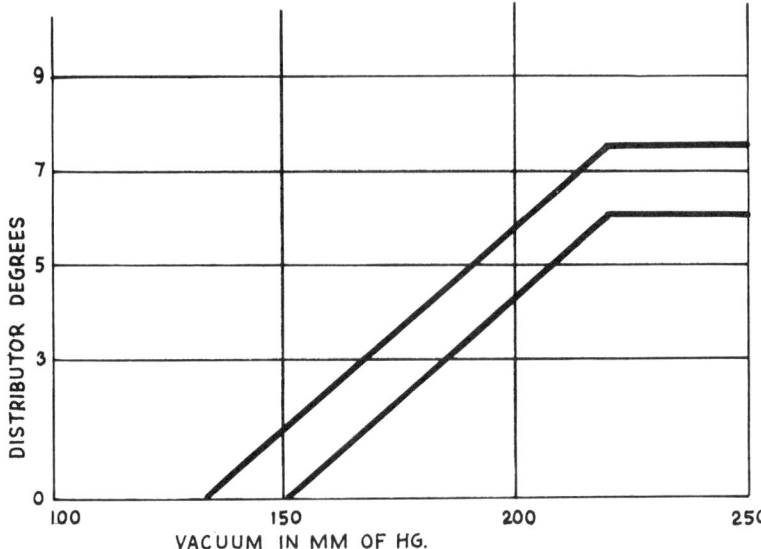

Vacuum advance of 1000 distributor.

Ignition and Distributor Specifications

Car Model	Timing °BTDC	Distributor — Point Gap In./MM.	Distributor — Breaker Spring Tension Ozs./Grs.	Centrifugal Advance — RPM	Centrifugal Advance — Degrees	Vacuum Advance — Hg	Vacuum Advance — Degrees	Dwell Angle°
1000	8°	.018–.021/.47–.53	18–21/500–600	425 2000	start 15	150 300	1 10	52–58
1204	6	.018–.020/.47–.53	21–24/600–700	450 2400	start 15	100(mm) 400(mm)	1 12	55–57
Simca 5		.017–.019/.43–.48	18–21/500–600	300 2000	start 11			55–57

° 12°, starting with 1963 engines.

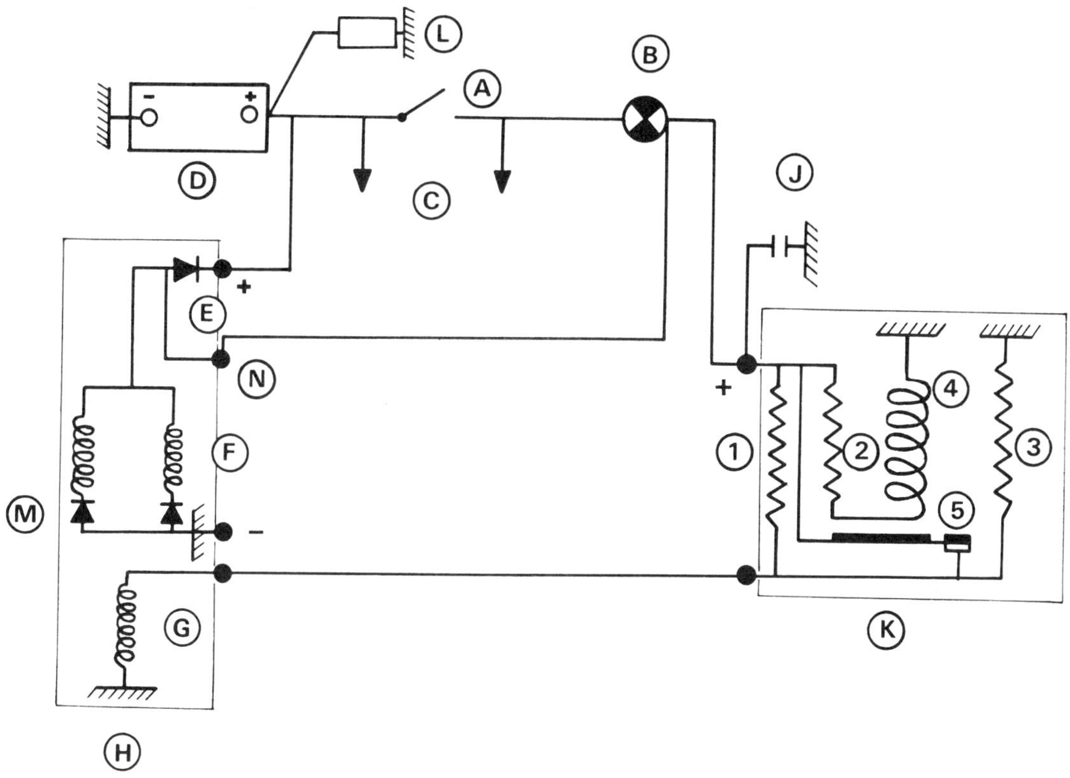

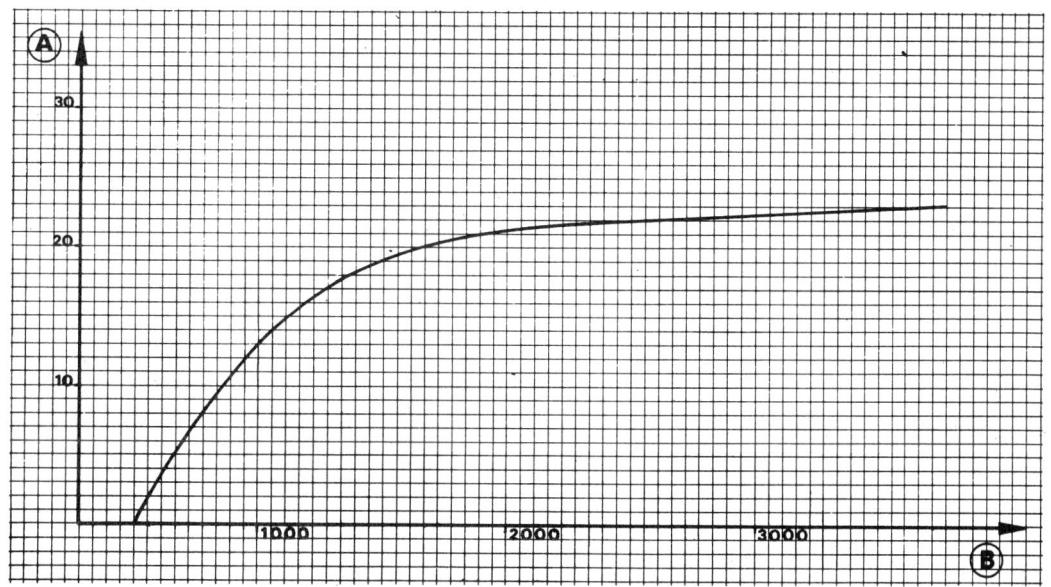

Simca 1204 battery charging components and interconnections.

1	Adjusting resistor	C	Consumers	J	Warning light protecting
2	Compensating resistor	D	Battery		condenser
3	Absorbing resistor	E	Insulating diode	K	Regulator
4	Relay	F	Stator	L	Starter motor
5	Contact	G	Rotor	M	Rectifier diodes
A	Contact	H	Alternator	N	Auxiliary terminal
B	Charge warning-light				

Normal alternator output current in amperes (A) for alternator rpm (B).

battery through the charge warning light and the ignition switch. And, the alternator receives excitation voltage from the battery only when the ignition switch is on.

Operation of the regulator is such that when the voltage is relatively low across the relay coil (4), the contacts (5) are closed, feeding excitation voltage directly to the alternator and raising the alternator output. When the voltage at the relay coil is sufficient to open the contacts, reduced excitation voltage is fed through the adjusting resistor (1), decreasing alternator output. The absorbing resistor (3) minimizes arcing at the relay terminals. The temperature compensating resistor (2) stabilizes relay operation, and the 470 microfarad condenser (J) protects the charge warning light from surges of high voltage.

Charging Equipment Tests

Before accurate tests can be made, it is necessary to temperature stabilize the electrical components by allowing the engine to run at fast idling speed (1200 rpm) for about 30 minutes. Tests require a 10-ohm, 500-watt rheostat, a 30-ampere DC ammeter and an 25-volt DC voltmeter.

Alternator output check. With the engine stopped, connect a shorting wire between the + BAT and EXC terminals of the regulator. Remove the lead from the alternator + terminal and connect it to the negative terminal of the test ammeter. Connect the positive terminal of the ammeter to the + terminal of the alternator.

CAUTION: prevent lead from touching ground since this is a hot lead from the battery. Never operate alternator with its + Battery terminal open.

Connect the positive terminal of the voltmeter to the + terminal of the alternator and the negative terminal to ground. Connect the rheostat between the negative terminal of the ammeter and ground.

Start the engine, run at 1000, 2000, and 3000 rpm and note the ammeter reading with the rheostat adjusted for a reading of 14 volts on the voltmeter for each speed. Current densities should be as follows:

Engine Speed	Amperes at 14 volts
1000 rpm	at least 12
2000 rpm	at least 20
3000 rpm	at least 22

If readings are lower than above in these tests, the diodes are probably defective and the alternator should be replaced.

Regulator check. With engine stopped, remove test wire used to short-circuit regulator + BAT and EXC terminals in the alternator check. Remove voltmeter from alternator + terminal and connect it between the regulator + BAT terminal and ground.

Start engine and run at 2750 rpm. Adjust alternator output to 15 amperes by means of the rheostat. The reading of the voltmeter should be between 14.7 and 15.3 volts. Gradually increase engine speed, keeping current at 15 amperes by adjusting the rheostat. The regulated voltage should remain in range and within 0.2 volts. Decrease engine speed to 2750 rpm and adjust current to 20 amperes with the rheostat. Voltage should stay between 14.7 and 15.3 volts. If voltage is not maintained within these limits, replace regulator.

Charge warning light check. When the ignition is switched on, the charge warning light glows, being fed from the battery with its return circuit through the regulator and alternator inductor windings. When the engine starts, voltage appearing at the + terminal of the alternator balances-out the voltage fed to the charge warning light and the light goes out. If the light does not go out, first check the condition of the wire and connections to the alternator auxiliary

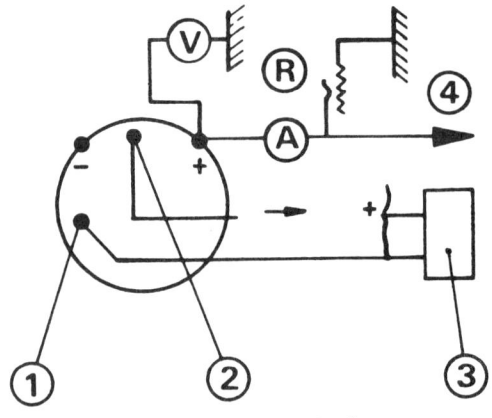

Alternator output check.

1 Excitation	A Ammeter
2 Auxiliary terminal	V Voltmeter
3 Regulator	R Rheostat
4 To battery +	
terminal	

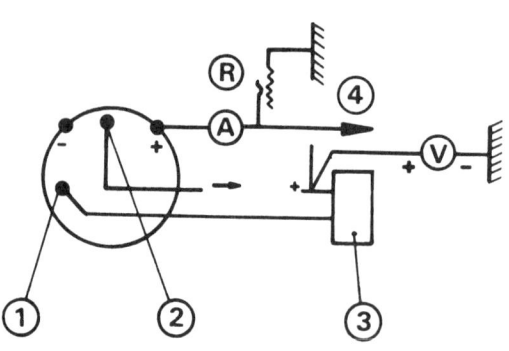

Alternator output check.

1 Excitation
2 Auxiliary terminal
3 Regulator
4 To battery +
  terminal

A Ammeter
V Voltmeter
R Rheostat

terminal (N). When the ignition switch is on, 12 volts should be at the terminal. Check this with a voltmeter.

Alternator Replacement

To remove alternator, disconnect battery and loosen alternator mounting and adjusting screws. Remove driving belt and disconnect four wires from alternator. Remove mounting screws and alternator from under car.

To install unit, place alternator tip in bracket and slide long bolt through holes. Attach adjusting strap to cylinder block and to alternator after inserting square plate into slide. Install driving belt over pulleys of crankshaft, water pump and alternator. Adjust belt tension by first scribing two marks on the slackened belt 3.93 in. (100 mm.) apart. Then move alternator in the adjustment strap to stretch belt until the two marks are 4.08 in. (104 mm.) apart. Lock adjusting strap screws.

CAUTION: never perform arc welding on a car fitted with an alternator without first disconnecting the alternator wiring.

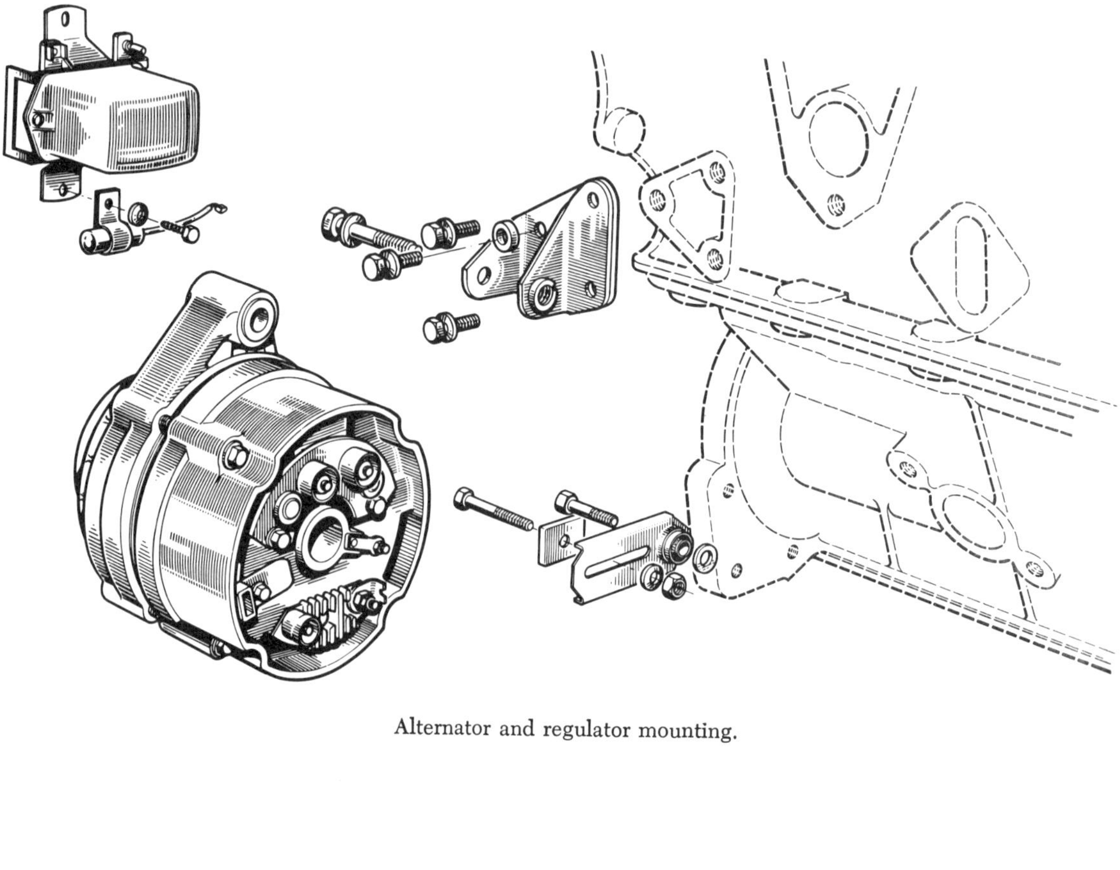

Alternator and regulator mounting.

Charging Equipment

Simca 1000

Battery charging components of the Simca 1000 cars include a Paris-Rhone DC generator and a Paris-Rhone Type YTD21 or YTD 219 DC regulator. The YTD21 regulator is used with the G10R34 generator and the YTD219 regulator is used with the G10C25 generator.

DC Generator

The DC generator has a rotating armature with copper windings that intersect lines of magnetic force between magnetic field poles. At the start, the magnetic field is weak because it is only residual. However, as current flows from the armature windings, part of the flow is fed into and excites the magnetic field. Increasing speed intensifies the magnetic field and thereby increases the voltage from the windings. Finally, the magnetic field becomes saturated with energy and no further increase in armature speed will add to the output.

DC Regulator

Since voltage produced by the generator is in direct ratio to the product of armature speed and exciting current in the magnetic field, a constant output voltage can be easily maintained by making compensating adjustments to the exciting current. Armature speed is based on engine rpm and is therefore not independently controllable. The regulator maintains a constant voltage output by interrupting the exciting current.

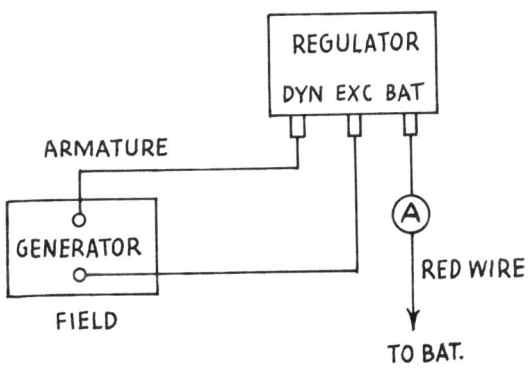

D.C. generator and regulator check.

Generator and Regulator Test

Before making tests on the generator or regulator, run the car engine at fast idle for about 30 minutes to temperature-stabilize the electrical components.

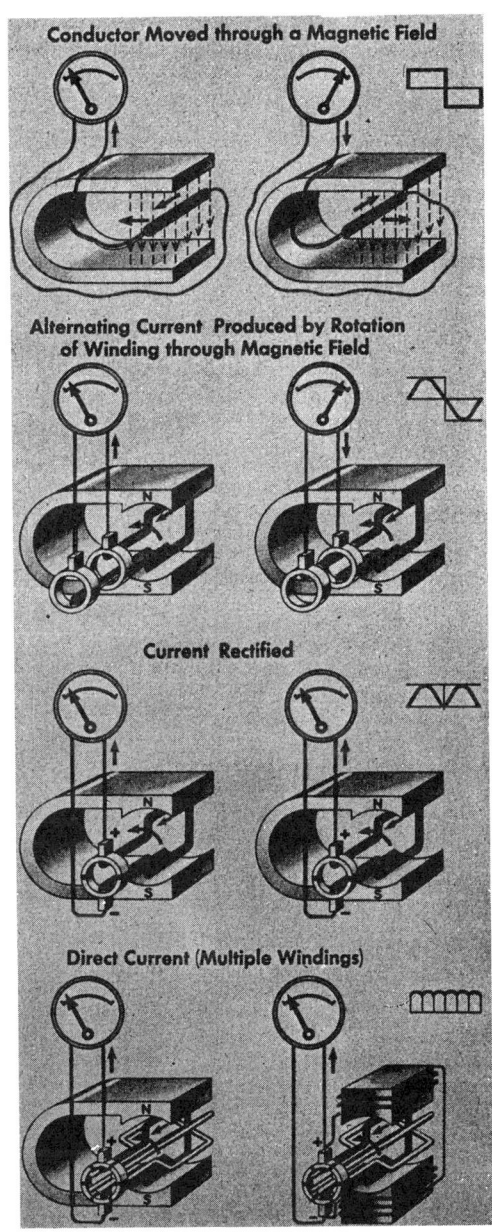

Generator windings intersect magnetic lines of force in opposite directions (as winding makes a complete revolution), causing an alternating current flow. In the d.c. generator, a segmented commutator on the armature shaft picks up current so that it flows in the same direction, rectifying the a.c. current. In the alternator there is no commutator, but the a.c. current is rectified by solid-state diodes.

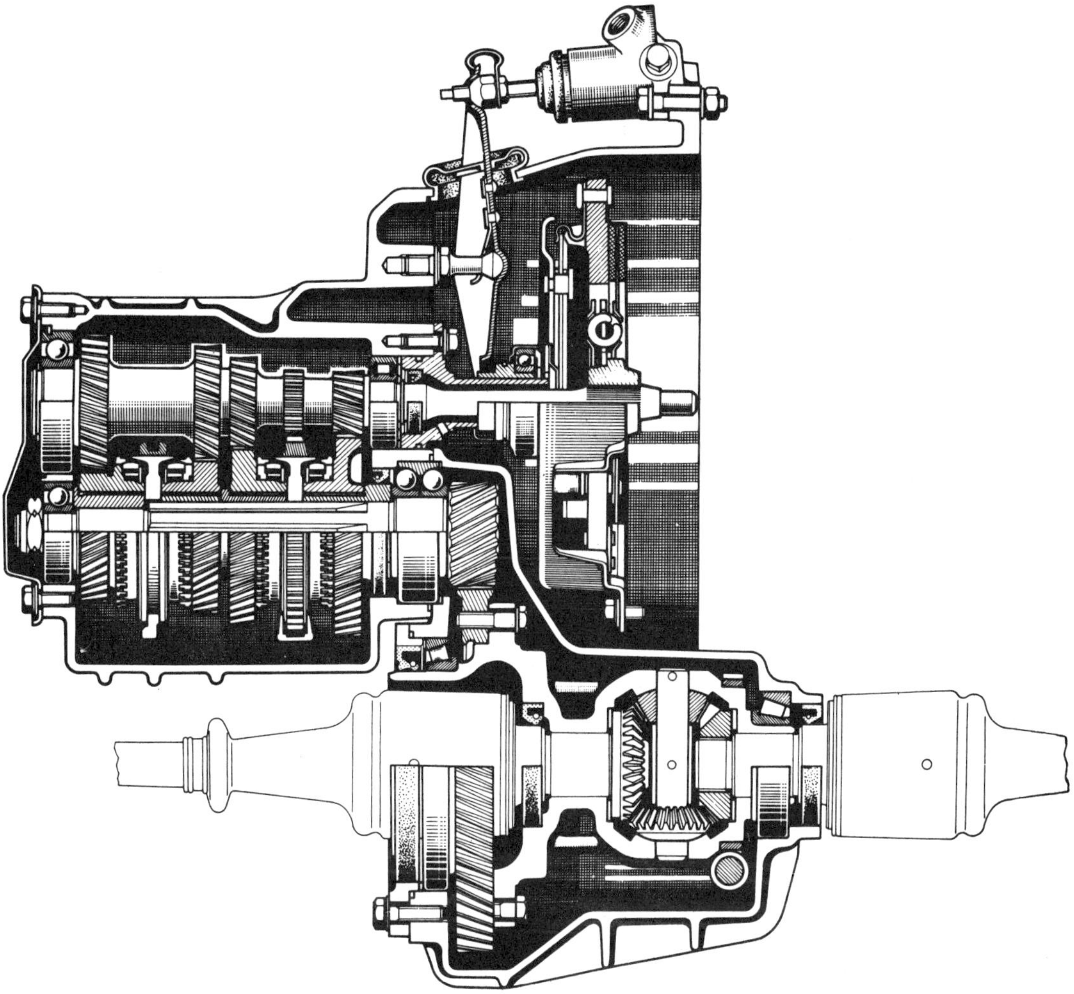

Simca 1204 transmission system.

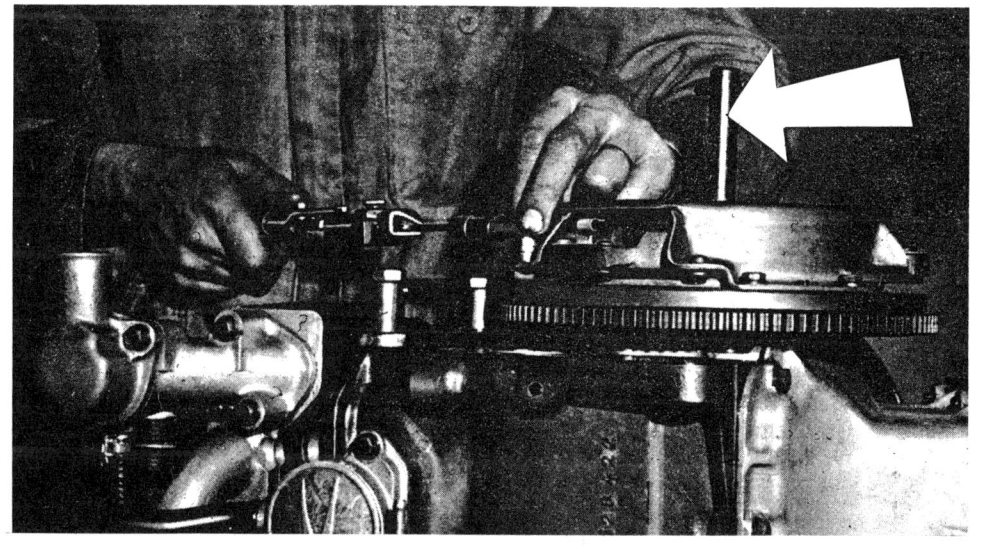

Use of dummy output shaft, tool PN20870E, to install clutch mechanism.

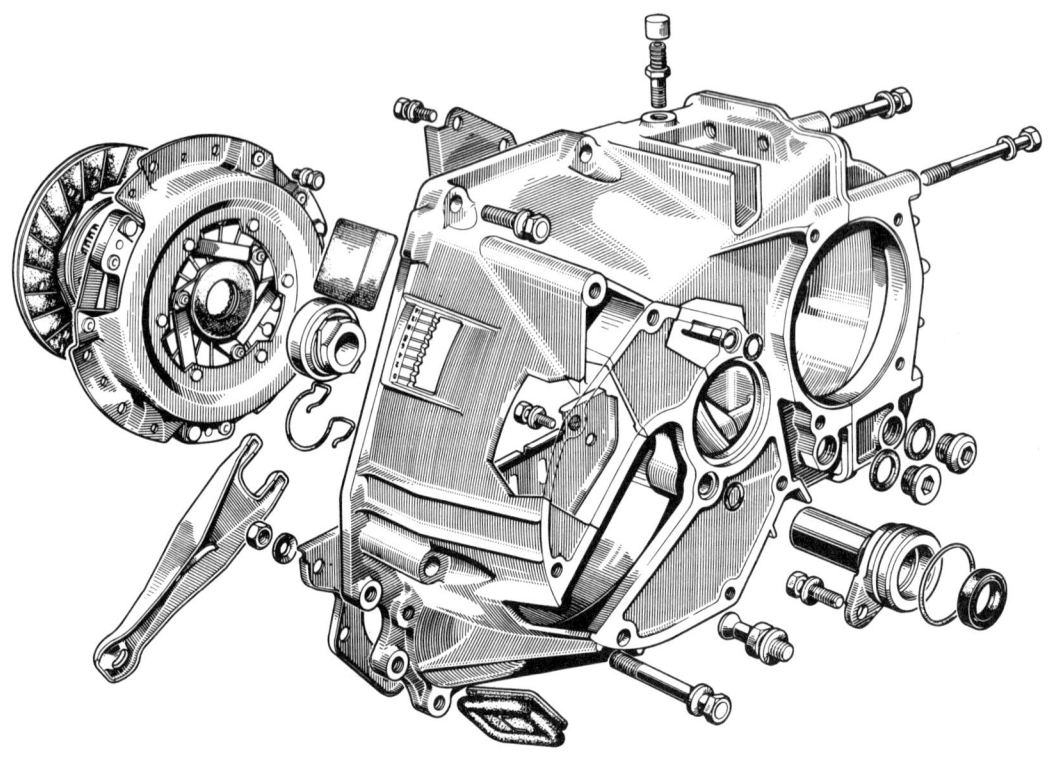

Simca 1204 clutch and housing.

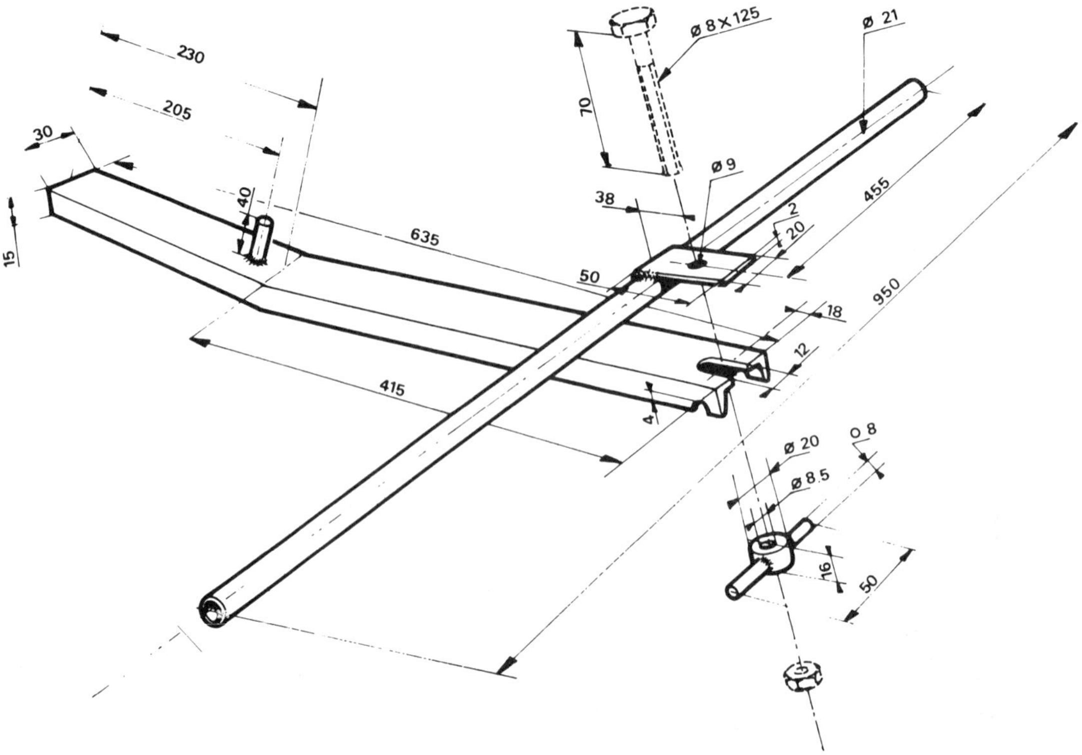

Engine holding bar to facilitate gearbox removal (dimensions in mm.).

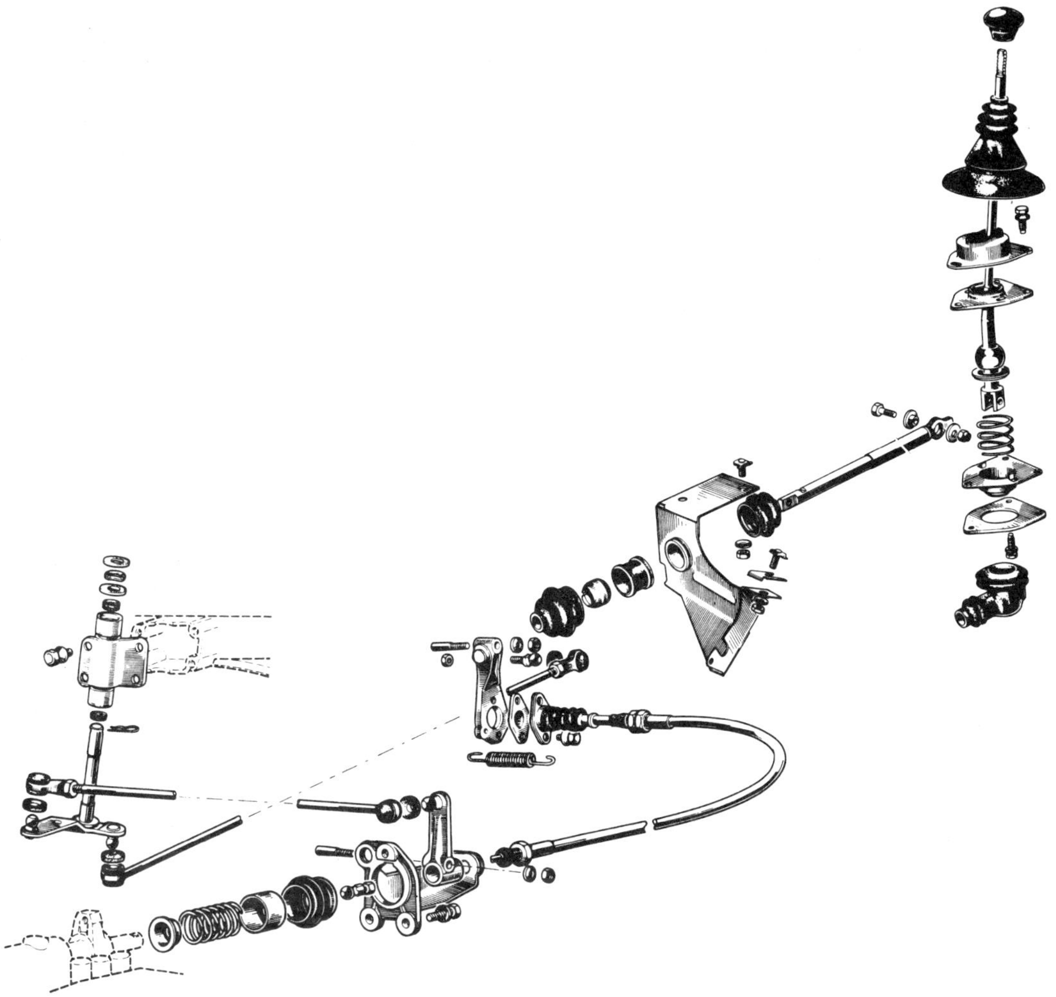

Gearshift and control linkage.

Installing engine holding bar.

Gearbox

Removal

Simca 1204

Disconnect battery terminals. Jack the front end of the car and place it on stands. Install engine holding bar. On cover side, remove gear shift control linkage and cable. Remove clutch slave cylinder and support the cylinder so that it is unnecesary to disconnect the fluid line. Remove left-hand front wheel and shock absorber and install suspension rod. Drain gearbox. Disassemble left-hand front engine mount and gearbox mount. Install two threaded pilot rods 2 in. (50 mm.) long by .31 in. (8 mm.) diameter in holes A (see illustration).

Remove remaining screws that hold gearbox and remove gearbox, collecting shims of drive-gear ball bearing for further use.

Installation

Simca 1204

Install the two pilots on the clutch housing, fit clutch fork on housing, and hold fork in de-clutched position with tie wire or strong rubber band. Engage one gear. Place shims of drive gear ball bearing into clutch housing, holding them in position with grease. Make sure that two small seals are fitted to the gearbox-to-front axle oil ways. Engage the release ball bearing into clutch housing.

Push gearbox input shaft into clutch while turning drive gear to engage shaft grooves. Slide gearbox over two pilot rods and position to fit drive gear on ring gear. Tighten screws and remove pilot rods. Place engine mount on gearbox using spacer between engine mount and clutch housing. Attach engine mount and remove holding bar. Mount clutch slave cylinder. Install gearshift linkage, cable, and then adjust. Replace shock absorber and wheel. Refill gearbox, check oil level in front axle and connect battery terminals.

Disassembly

Simca 1204

Remove control cover and rear cover and engage two gears to lock the gearbox. Remove left-hand threaded drive gear locknut, and remove gear by sliding through other gears (adapter counterplate positioned by the four mounting screws of the gearbox rear cover). Leave adapter counterplate and puller PN39962K in position and remove third and fourth speed gears, synchronizer, and rings. Remove drive gear rear ball bearing, pushing it into the gearbox. Leaving adapter counterplate in place, remove reverse slide gear circlip, collar pin, shaft, and slide gear.

Remove the release bearing bracket that butts against the roller bearing of the primary shaft. Recover shims and remove circlip of primary shaft roller bearing. With tool PN20888, remove primary shaft and two bearings. Using puller PN15525F, remove outer cage with rollers of primary

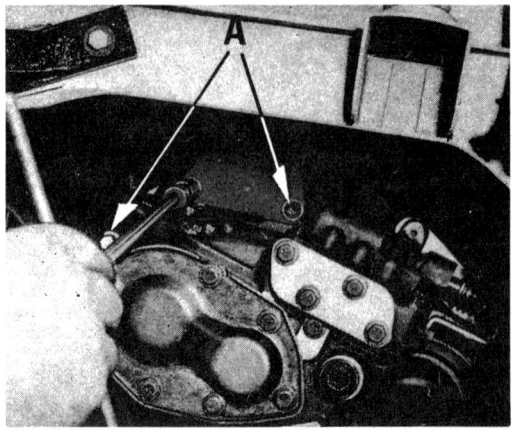

Installing two pilot rods.

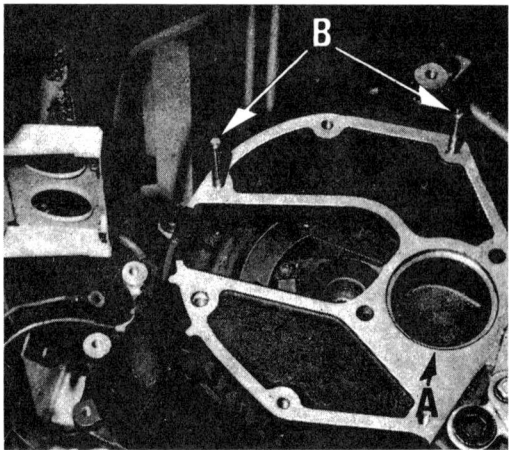

Drive gear ball bearing shims (A), pilot rods (B).

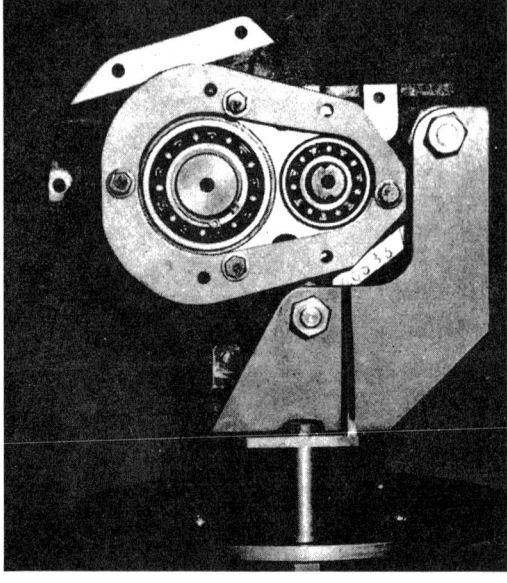

Positioning of tool PN20897N.

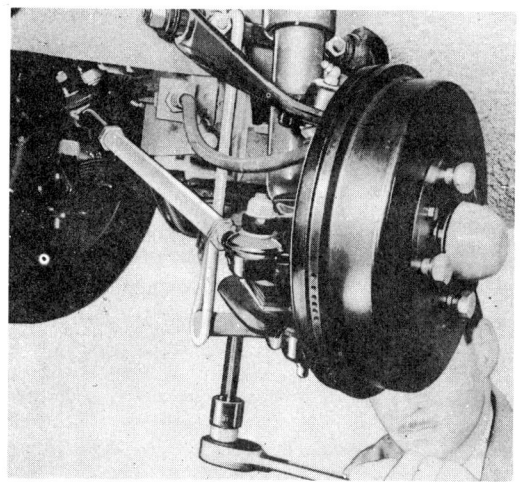

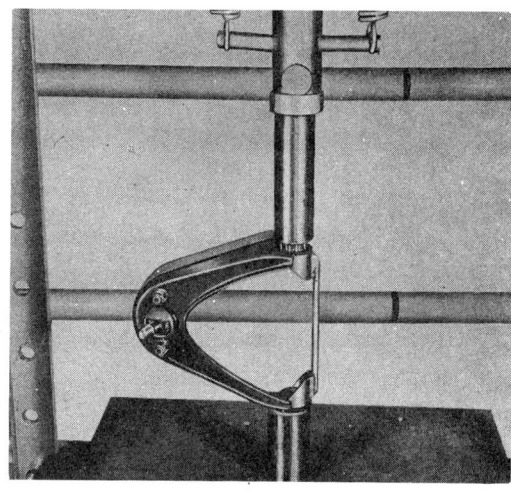

Use of spacer prevents bending of suspension arm when fitting bushings.

Suspension Arm Disassembly

Remove nuts and washers from rubber bushings. Remove ruber bushings with tool PN39955L and remove pin. Check that bores of suspension arm do not exceed 1.123 in. (28.5 mm.). Use a spacer to keep from bending suspension arm when press fitting new bushings. Insert one bushing, then install pin and insert second bushing. Install washers and nuts but do not tighten completely until car is jacked down and bushings are under load to assume their proper position.

Front Suspension Removal

Jack car and place on stands.

WARNING: a stand must also be placed under the rear crossmember of the engine to keep the car from tilting backward when front suspension is removed.

Remove wheels. From inside front compartment, remove steering box inspection cover. Remove screws holding steering gear housing to floor. Disconnect housing from control rod by removing screw and bushing. Remove control rod. Install spring compressor PN39972 and compress to maximum. Remove screws holding steering box and idler arm to frame. Disconnect shock absorbers from frame. Disconnect brake lines and plug the lines. Remove suspension arm from frame and support front suspension assembly. Remove rubber spring supports from each side. Remove front sus-

Suspension arm removal.

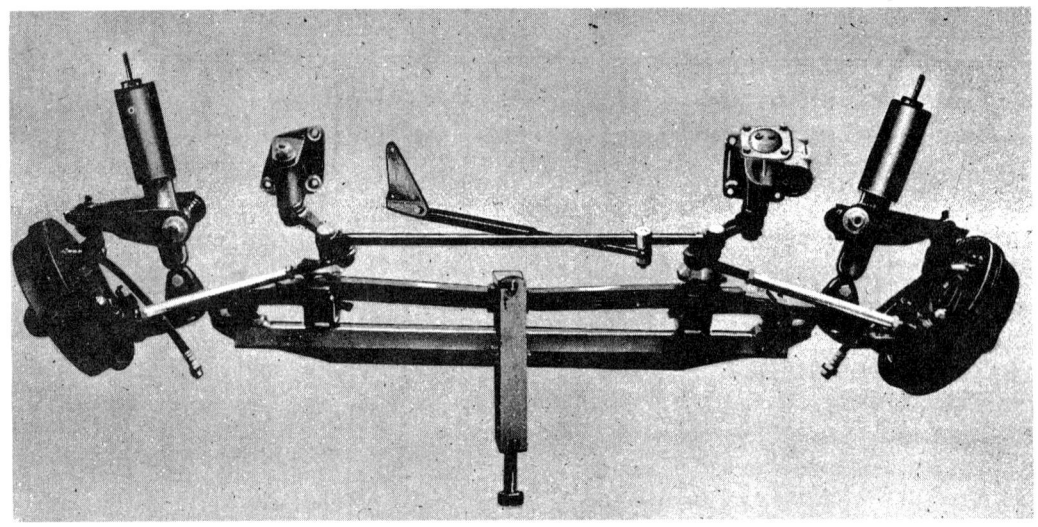

Front suspension and steering assembly removed.

pension and steering assembly with spring compressor in place.

Steering Gear

Simca 1000

The steering is a Gemmer cam and roller type with a gear ratio of 13:1 and turning radius of 14.7 ft. (4.5 M). Linkage ball joints require no lubrication, but the ball joints mounted on the spring and front suspension arm should be lubricated every 12,000 miles.

Steering Box Removal

Remove inspection cover for access to steering box. Disconnect box from shaft by removing lock screw (1). Remove steering shaft (2) and ball joint nuts (3). Remove two ball joints with puller PN4028W. Remove mounting screws (4), plate, lockwashers, and steering box.

Steering Check and Adjustment

First check for the cause of any abnormal play in the steering assembly by jacking the front wheels and inspecting the linkage while the steering wheel is being moved. If the linkage and ball joints appear to be in good condition, turn wheels straight ahead and drop arm from steering drag link to check steering box. Lock steering wheel

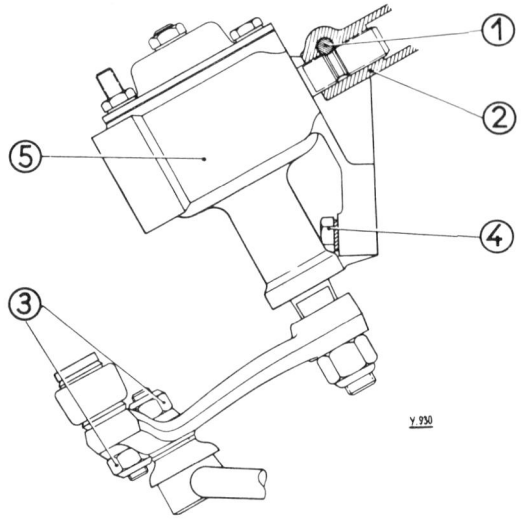

Steering box assembly.

at various positions and check steering arm for play by moving arm back and forth. Excessive bearing play in the steering shaft will be evidenced by some side motion. If steering arm shows play, loosen locknut on the steering box and turn adjustment screw until play is at a maximum for all positions of the steering wheel. Tighten locknut. Return steering wheel to straight-ahead driving position and reconnect steering arm.

Overtightening of the screw in the steering column support in some cases may cause binding of the steering shaft in cer-

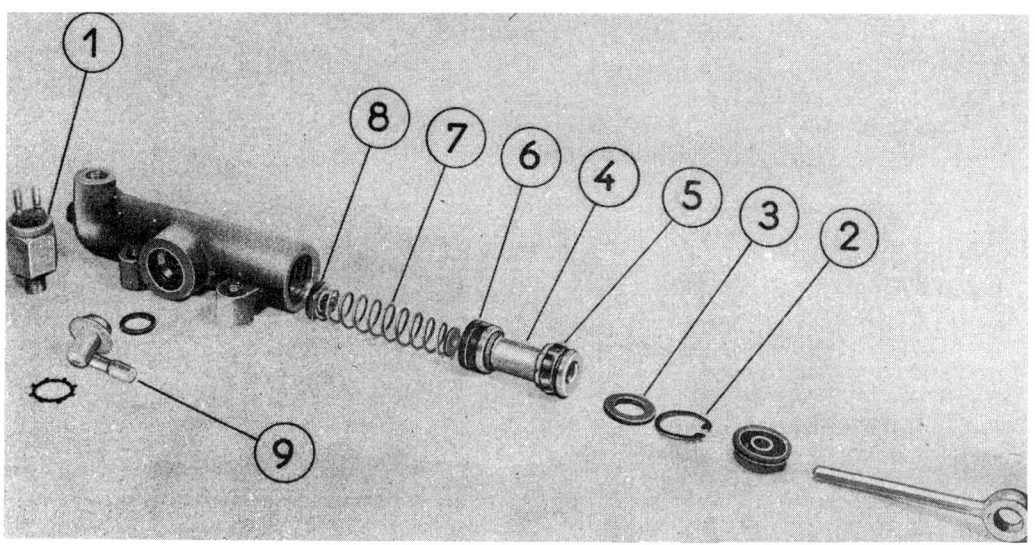

Brake master cylinder components.

tain positions of the wheel. To correct this, remove screw and insert a washer.

Brake System

Simca 1000

Drum brakes on front and rear are hydraulically operated, except handbrake which mechanically controls the two rear wheels and is independent of the foot brake system.

Master Cylinder Overhaul

Drain the brake system. Disconnect battery cable. Disconnect stoplight wires and lines from master cylinder. Remove mounting screws and master cylinder.

Disassemble master cylinder by removing the following parts in the order given:
  a. Brake stoplight switch (1)
  b. Lockring (2)
  c. Thrust washer (3)
  d. Piston (4)
  e. Secondary cup (5)
  f. Primary cup (6)
  g. Spring (7)
  h. Pressure valve (8)
  i. Master cylinder feedline connection (9).

Inspect master cylinder bore and clean with brake fluid and a brush. Check bypass and compensating parts for restric-tions. Dip all parts in brake fluid and, taking particular care to keep parts clean, reassemble in reverse order from removal. Check for free operation and test for proper seating of lockring.

Brake Cylinder Removal

Remove brake drum after marking drum and hub for proper reassembly. Detach upper spring from brake shoes. Disconnect hydraulic line, remove screws and wheel cylinder. To reassemble, reverse the sequence and bleed hydraulic system.

Foot Brake Adjustment

If brake pedal is spongy, brake system should be bled and adjusted. To adjust, jack wheel and turn eccentric cam of each brake shoe until lining is tight against the drum. Then turn cams in reverse direction

Tighten brakes by turning cams in directions shown.

until wheel just turns freely. Brake pedal free play should be between .079 in. and .394 in. (2–10 mm.) and is adjusted by bending the stop on the pedal support.

Handbrake Adjustment

With foot brakes adjusted, the handbrake is adjusted by loosening the locknut on the control rod and turning the adjusting nut to tighten the cable. Progressively tighten brake with each ratchet notch so that total lock of rear wheels is obtained on the sixth or seventh notch of the ratchet.

Wheel Alignment

Simca 1000

Proper alignment of front and rear suspension systems is important to good tire mileage and ease of car handling. Front and rear wheel alignment specifications are given in the tables. The front spring is compressed with tool PN39972M, while the rear suspension is compressed by clamps. Changes made in rear wheel alignment make it necessary to check front wheel alignment. Therefore, when checking and adjusting a car after an accident, always begin with the rear wheels. Check with rear tire pressure at 15.6 and front at 24.2 psi.

Rear Wheel Camber Adjustment

Check rear wheel alignment after adjusting camber since changes in camber affect

Camber adjustment using shims.

toe-in. Adjust camber by use of shims under the two bolts that hold the suspension arm pin to the crossmember. Adding shims decreases camber and removing shims increases camber. Total thickness of shims should never exceed .118 in. (2.99 mm.).

Rear Wheel Alignment

Rear wheels must be parallel to the centerline of the car, and there should be no toe-in or toe-out with the car standing empty and on a level surface. If measured toe-in or toe-out is small, correction may be made by loosening the nuts that hold the rear suspension arms to the crossmember, then prying the suspension arm assembly in the direction required. The oversize holes in the pins allow some movement. Tighten nuts and re-check alignment. If the correction is insufficient, it will be necessary to make the adjustment by adding or removing shims as in an adjusting camber. As mentioned, these two adjustment are interacting.

With the rear wheels aligned, (no toe-in or toe-out), check that they are parallel with the centerline of the car. Any necessary adjustment is made by first loosening the crossmember from the front engine mount and from the frame of the car, then raising the car body slightly to allow movement of the crossmember to correct misalignment, and re-tightening the screws.

Front Wheel Caster Adjustment

Caster, camber, and toe-in should be adjusted in that order. Caster is adjusted by use of shims under the rear mounting screw of the upper suspension arm. Adjust caster to specifications for car model. Changes in caster adjustment affect camber.

Front Wheel Camber Adjustment

With caster adjustment correct, adjust camber to specifications by adding or removing the same thickness of shims under the two screws that hold the upper suspension arm to the body. Tighten screws and re-check camber. Changes in camber adjustment will alter toe-in.

Front Wheel Toe-in Adjustment

With camber adjusted, check toe-in and make any necessary adjustment by loosening the locknut on the tie rod and turning the rod to change its length for proper toe-in. Tighten locknut after toe-in is correct.

Rear Suspension

Simca 1000

The independent rear wheel suspension system uses coil springs and requires no lubrication. It is attached to the car frame and to the triangular crossmember which supports the front end of the power plant.

Rear Suspension Removal

Remove power plant and rear crossmember as described in Chapter Three, and disconnect handbrake cable near the handbrake. Remove cover fasteners and disconnect brake hydraulic system. Remove front screws holding crossmember to body. Disconnect lug between body and rear suspension crossmember. Remove rear suspension.

When re-installing rear suspension, position PN39952R on rear crossmember and body to hold it in place while mounting screws are started. Bleed brake system and check rear wheel alignment.

Use of bar to position rear suspension to start mounting screws.

Rear Suspension Arm Removal

Either rear suspension arm can be removed without the entire assembly. Place car on stands and remove wheel. Discon-nect half-axle from wheel hub. Support arm with a jack to compress the spring. Remove shock absorber and disconnect brake line from suspension arm. Remove jack to decompress spring and remove spring, plate and insulator. Remove brake drum. Disconnect handbrake cable by removing cover retainer which is press fitted on brake drum. Remove screws holding armshaft to crossmember, and remove suspension arm assembly.

Re-install rear suspension arm assembly by reversing the removal procedure. Bleed brake system and check rear wheel alignment. If wheels are misaligned, check for improper positioning of the crossmember (see REAR WHEEL ALIGNMENT).

Rear Wheel Half-Axle Removal

Jack rear of car and place on stands. On the wheel side of the shaft, remove four screws from flange and pull flange. Pull half-axle and remove rubber bushing. From transaxle side, remove clip and cap, and pull shaft downward with two blocks. Re-install by reversing above procedure, remembering to install rubber bushing before assembling flange. Use tool PN39968Z to position half-axle with two blocks in the planetary gear opening.

Rear Wheel Bearing Adjustment

Rear wheel bearing preload is provided by a collapsible spacer located between the bearing races. To obtain the proper preload, progressively tighten the locknut while rotating the wheel several times to seat the bearings. Torque to between .43 and .72 ft. lbs. (60–100 m/kgm.). Do not overtighten or it will be necessary to replace the collapsible spacer. Bleed hydraulic brake system and check rear wheel alignment.

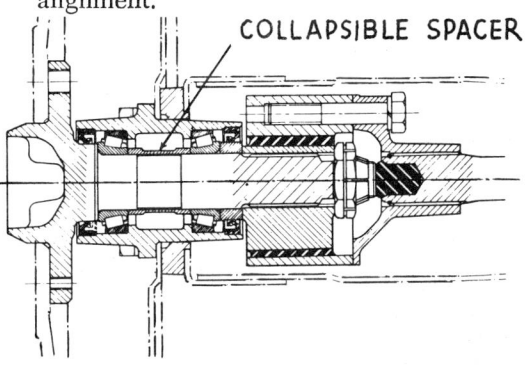

Rear wheel bearing adjustment.

Appendix

Conversion—Metric and American Measure

Linear Units (distance, length, angle)

1 kilometer	= 0.6214 miles or 3,280 feet
1 mile	= 1.6093 kilometers

Multiply kilometers by 0.6214 to get miles
Multiply miles by 1.6093 to get kilometers

1 kilometer	= 1000 meters
1 meter	= 3.281 feet or 39.370 inches
1 centimeter	= 0.394 inches
1 inch	= 2.540 centimeters

Multiply centimeters by 0.394 to get inches
Multiply inches by 2.54 to get centimeters

1 degree (1°)	= 60 minutes (60')
1 minute (1')	= 60 second (60")

Cubic Units (volume, displacement)

1 liter	= 1000 cubic centimeters = 61.022 cubic inches
1 cubic centimeter (milliliter)	= 0.061 cubic inches
1 cubic inch	= 16.387 cubic centimeters

Multiply cubic centimeters by 0.61 to get cubic inches
Multiply cubic inches by 16.387 to get cubic centimeters

1 liter = 0.264 gallons = 1.057 quarts = 2.1 pints
1 gallon = 3.784 liters = 231 cubic inches
Multiply liters by 0.264 to get gallons
Multiply gallons by 231 to get cubic inches

Engine Displacement

Cubic-inch displacement is found by multiplying the bore by itself; multiplying this answer by 0.7854; multiplying this answer by the stroke; and multiplying this answer by the number of cylinders.

The constant 0.7854 is used rather than π (the mathematical constant, 3.14159) because the bore of the cylinder is the diameter, not the radius. Using π, the formula is:

$$\left(\frac{\text{bore}}{2}\right)^2 \times \pi \times (\text{stroke}) \times (\text{\# cylinders}) = \text{displacement}$$

The same formula is used to determine the displacement of an engine in metric units (centimeters), but only after the millimeter bore and stroke dimensions are changed to centimeters. Change millimeters to centimeters by dividing by ten.

Force Units (pressure, torque)

1 atmosphere (atm)	= 14.7 pounds per square inch (psi)
1 pound per square inch	= 0.068 atmosphere

Pressure is measured as force against a surface, not volume. A bicycle tire at 50 psi has far less air in it than a car tire having 17 psi.

1 kilogram per square centimeter	= 14.223 pounds per square inch
1 kilogram-meter	= 7.233 foot-pounds

A foot-pound is a unit of force equal to one pound raised one foot high.

An inch-pound is one pound raised one inch high.

British Imperial Measures In Cubic Inches

	Imperial	U. S.
Gallon	277.4	231
Quart	69.4	57.8
Pint	34.7	28.9

Gasoline Consumption By Miles and Kilometers

1 mile per gallon	= 0.355 kilometers per liter
30 miles per gallon	= 10.64 kilometers per liter
1 kilometer per liter	= 2.82 miles per gallon
8 kilometers per liter	= 22.6 miles per gallon

Common Automotive Abbreviations

L	= liters (measurement of volume) or Luxor (meaning deluxe)
mm	= millimeters
cc	= cubic centimeters
ohv	= overhead valves
CIH	= camshaft in cylinder head (rocker arm required)
ohc	= overhead camshaft (no rocker arm needed)
OEM	= original equipment manufactured
bhp	= brake horsepower
SAE	= Society of Automotive Engineers
DIN	= German Engineering Norms
rpm	= revolutions per minute
ft. lbs.	= foot pounds (units of force)
in. lbs.	= inch pounds
POE	= port of entry
A.I.R.	= air injection reactor (exhaust emission control system)

Conversion—Millimeters to Decimal Inches

mm	inches	mm	inches	mm	inches	mm	inches	mm	inches
1	.039 370	31	1.220 470	61	2.401 570	91	3.582 670	210	8.267 700
2	.078 740	32	1.259 840	62	2.440 940	92	3.622 040	220	8.661 400
3	.118 110	33	1.299 210	63	2.480 310	93	3.661 410	230	9.055 100
4	.157 480	34	1.338 580	64	2.519 680	94	3.700 780	240	9.448 800
5	.196 850	35	1.377 949	65	2.559 050	95	3.740 150	250	9.842 500
6	.236 220	36	1.417 319	66	2.598 420	96	3.779 520	260	10.236 200
7	.275 590	37	1.456 689	67	2.637 790	97	3.818 890	270	10.629 900
8	.314 960	38	1.496 050	68	2.677 160	98	3.858 260	280	11.032 600
9	.354 330	39	1.535 430	69	2.716 530	99	3.897 630	290	11.417 300
10	.393 700	40	1.574 800	70	2.755 900	100	3.937 000	300	11.811 000
11	.433 070	41	1.614 170	71	2.795 270	105	4.133 848	310	12.204 700
12	.472 440	42	1.653 540	72	2.834 640	110	4.330 700	320	12.598 400
13	.511 810	43	1.692 910	73	2.874 010	115	4.527 550	330	12.992 100
14	.551 180	44	1.732 280	74	2.913 380	120	4.724 400	340	13.385 800
15	.590 550	45	1.771 650	75	2.952 750	125	4.921 250	350	13.779 500
16	.629 920	46	1.811 020	76	2.992 120	130	5.118 100	360	14.173 200
17	.669 290	47	1.850 390	77	3.031 490	135	5.314 950	370	14.566 900
18	.708 660	48	1.889 760	78	3.070 860	140	5.511 800	380	14.960 600
19	.748 030	49	1.929 130	79	3.110 230	145	5.708 650	390	15.354 300
20	.787 400	50	1.968 500	80	3.149 600	150	5.905 500	400	15.748 000
21	.826 770	51	2.007 870	81	3.188 970	155	6.102 350	500	19.685 000
22	.866 140	52	2.047 240	82	3.228 340	160	6.299 200	600	23.622 000
23	.905 510	53	2.086 610	83	3.267 710	165	6.496 050	700	27.559 000
24	.944 880	54	2.125 980	84	3.307 080	170	6.692 900	800	31.496 000
25	.984 250	55	2.165 350	85	3.346 450	175	6.889 750	900	35.433 000
26	1.023 620	56	2.204 720	86	3.385 820	180	7.086 600	1000	39.370 000
27	1.062 990	57	2.244 090	87	3.425 190	185	7.283 450	2000	78.740 000
28	1.102 360	58	2.283 460	88	3.464 560	190	7.480 300	3000	118.110 000
29	1.141 730	59	2.322 830	89	3.503 903	195	7.677 150	4000	157.480 000
30	1.181 100	60	2.362 200	90	3.543 300	200	7.874 000	5000	196.850 000

To change decimal millimeters to decimal inches, position the decimal point where desired on either side of the millimeter measurement shown and reset the inches decimal by the same number of digits in the same direction. For example, to convert .001 mm into decimal inches, reset the decimal behind the 1 mm (shown on the chart) to .001; change the decimal inch equivalent (.039″ shown) to .00039″.

Multiple Terminology for Automobile Parts

In some cases there is more than one name for an automobile part or assembly. Equivalent meanings are given below. "Br." stands for British.

Carburetor

air correction jet (Br.), high-speed air bleed
butterfly, throttle valve, throttle plate
choke tube (Br.), venturi
emulsion tube (Br.), main vent tube
idle speed screw, throttle stop screw
main jet (Br.), main metering jet
pilot jet (Br.), idling jet
pilot jet air bleed (Br.), idle air adjusting screw
progression circuit (Br.), second idle stage
slow-running adjustment (Br.), idle speed adjustment
slow-running volume adjustment (Br.), idle mixture adjustment
strangler (Br.), choke

Engine

bearing insert, bearing shell, bearing
core plug (Br.), welsh plug, drain plug
crankpin, journal
gudgeon pin (Br.), piston pin, wrist pin
retaining clip, circlip, snap ring
scraper ring, oil ring
clutch driven plate, drive disc
oil sump, oil pan
slave cylinder, servo cylinder, operating cylinder

Electrical

alternator, a.c. generator
dynamo (Br.), generator
earth (Br.), ground
distributor shaft, driving spindle

Suspension

kingpin slant, steering knuckle inclination, swivel
  axle angle
control arm, control link
crossmember, assembly member

Miscellaneous

filling up, topping up
bushings, bushes, shell bearings
fork, yoke
brake backing plate, securing plate

Tightening Specifications

Simca 1204

Engine and Block

	Ft. Lbs./Kgm.
Alternator on bracket	36/5
Air cleaner on carburetor	8/1
Alternator bracket on block	14/2
Adjusting strap on alternator	14/2
Adjusting strap on oil pan	14/2
Breather on cylinder block	8.6/1
Cylinder block drain plug	12/1.7
Carburetor on manifold	14/2
Camshaft flange	10.8/1.5
Connecting rod big end cap	26.7/3.7

Crankshaft main bearing cap	47/6.5
Cylinder head on cylinder block	47/6.5
Clutch mechanism on flywheel	8/1
Crankshaft pulley	61/8.5
Camshaft gear	10.8/1.5
Center engine mount on engine	15.9/2
Center engine mount on leaf	8.6/1
Center rubber support on crossmember	15.9/2
Center rubber support on bracket and crossmember	8.6/1
Crown gear and diaphragm converter	26.7/3.7
Distributor	7/1
Distributor bracket on block	14/2
Diaphragm on crankshaft (Ferodo)	39.7/5.5
Exhaust manifold on cylinder head	14/2
Exhaust strainer on cylinder block	8.6/1
Extension on oil pan	7/1
Fuel pump on cylinder block	14/2
Flywheel on crankshaft	39.7/5.5
Intake manifold on cylinder head	10.8/1.5
Left-hand engine mount on clutch housing	15.9/2
Left-hand engine rubber support on side member	36/5
Left-hand engine rubber support on steel sheet bracket	15.9/2
Oil pan drain plug	25/3.5
Oil pan on cylinder block	8.6/1
Oil pressure switch on cylinder block	25/3.5
Oil pump and cover on cylinder block	8/1
Oil dipstick bracket on block	8.6/1
Plug, oil pump valve	19.5/2.7
Rocker arm cover on cylinder head	5/0.7

Conversion—Common Fractions to Decimals and Millimeters

Common Fractions	Inches Decimal Fractions	Millimeters (approx.)	Common Fractions	Inches Decimal Fractions	Millimeters (approx.)	Common Fractions	Inches Decimal Fractions	Millimeters (approx.)
1/128	.008	0.20	11/32	.344	8.73	43/64	.672	17.07
1/64	.016	0.40	23/64	.359	9.13	11/16	.688	17.46
1/32	.031	0.79	3/8	.375	9.53	45/64	.703	17.86
3/64	.047	1.19	25/64	.391	9.92	23/32	.719	18.26
1/16	.063	1.59	13/32	.406	10.32	47/64	.734	18.65
5/64	.078	1.98	27/64	.422	10.72	3/4	.750	19.05
3/32	.094	2.38	7/16	.438	11.11	49/64	.766	19.45
7/64	.109	2.78	29/64	.453	11.51	25/32	.781	19.84
1/8	.125	3.18	15/32	.469	11.91	51/64	.797	20.24
9/64	.141	3.57	31/64	.484	12.30	13/16	.813	20.64
5/32	.156	3.97	1/2	.500	12.70	53/64	.828	21.03
11/64	.172	4.37	33/64	.516	13.10	27/32	.844	21.43
3/16	.188	4.76	17/32	.531	13.49	55/64	.859	21.83
13/64	.203	5.16	35/64	.547	13.89	7/8	.875	22.23
7/32	.219	5.56	9/16	.563	14.29	57/64	.891	22.62
15/64	.234	5.95	37/64	.578	14.68	29/32	.906	23.02
1/4	.250	6.35	19/32	.594	15.08	59/64	.922	23.42
17/64	.266	6.75	39/64	.609	15.48	15/16	.938	23.81
9/32	.281	7.14	5/8	.625	15.88	61/64	.953	24.21
19/64	.297	7.54	41/64	.641	16.27	31/32	.969	24.61
5/16	.313	7.94	21/32	.656	16.67	63/64	.984	25.00
21/64	.328	8.33						

Rocker arm, screw lock nut	12/1.7
Right-hand engine rubber support on side member	36/5
Right-hand engine rubber support on steel sheet bracket	15.9/2
Spark plug on cylinder head	21.6/3
Sealing shell on cylinder block	8.6/1
Starting motor on clutch housing	14/2
Timing gear cover on cylinder block	8.6/1
Temperature switch on cylinder head	10.8/1.5
Valve body in oil pump cover	26.7/3.7
Water outlet elbow cap	8.6/1
Water return manifold on cylinder block	14/2
Water inlet elbow on oil pan	8/1
Water outlet elbow on cylinder head	8/1
Water pump on oil pan	8/1
Water pump pulley	10.8/1.5
Cap to connecting rod big end	27/3.7
Cylinder head to block	47/6.5
Drive diaphragm to crankshaft (Ferodo option)	40/5.5
Flywheel to crankshaft	40/5.5
Pulley to crankshaft	61/8.5
Ring gear and diaphragm to converter (Ferodo option)	27/3.7
Rocker arm adjusting screws	12/1.7
Rocker cover to cylinder head	5/0.7
Timing gear cover to cylinder block	11/1.5
Timing wheel to camshaft	11/1.5
Breather pipe to cylinder block	9/1.2
Dipstick bracket to cylinder block	9/1.2
Extension to oil pan	7/1.0
Filtering element (hand tightened).	
Oil pump and cover to cylinder block	9/1.2
Oil drain plug to engine oil pan	25/3.5
Oil pan to cylinder block	9/1.2
Oil strainer	9/1.2
Sealing shell to cylinder block	9/1.2
Valve plug	20/2.7
Valve body	27/3.7

Fuel System

	Ft. Lbs./ Kgm.
Air cleaner to carburetor	9/1
Center attachment: suspension rings to car body	5/0.7
Center attachment: suspension rings to muffler circular bracket	7/1
Collar bracket of muffler, tightening	7/1
Carburetor to intake manifold	14/2
Exhaust manifold to cylinder head	14/2
Fuel pump to cylinder block	14/2
Fuel tank to car body	16/2
Front pipe to manifold	12/1.7
Front pipe to muffler inlet pipe	7/1
Half collar to front pipe	7/1
Intake manifold to cylinder head	11/1.5
Rear attachment: suspension rings to car body	5/0.7
Rear flange to outlet pipe	7/1
Suspension rings to attaching cross-member	5/0.7
Suspension rings to rear flange	7/1

Cooling System

	Ft. Lbs./ Kgm.
Cap to water outlet elbow	11/1.5
Electric motor to shroud	12/1.7

Expansion bottle to body	12/1.7
Fan to engine	18/2.5
Pulley to water pump	11/1.5
Radiator base part to body	12/1.7
Radiator top to body	12/1.7
Shroud upper part to body	12/1.7
Shroud lower part to body	12/1.7
Temperature switch to radiator	25/3.5
Water pump to engine oil sump	11/1.5
Water inlet elbow to engine oil sump	11/1.5
Water outlet elbow to cylinder head	11/1.5
Water return manifold to cylinder block	14/2.0

Electrical System

	Ft. Lbs./ Kgm.
Alternator to bracket	34/4.7
Alternator bracket to cylinder block	14/2
Adjusting strap to alternator	14/2
Adjusting strap to engine oil sump	14/2
Distributor bracket to cylinder block	14/2
Distributor	7/1
Oil pressure switch	25/3.5
Starting motor to clutch housing	14/2
Temperature switch	11/1.5

Spark Plugs:

	Ft. Lbs./ Kgm.
AC Delco, copper plated steel washer	22/3
Champion, cadmium plated steel washer	14/2
Marchal, flexible metal washer	22/3

Transmission System

	Ft. Lbs./ Kgm.
Ball joint to clutch housing	32/4.5
Clutch master cylinder to pedal bracket	7/1.0
Clutch mechanism to engine flywheel	11/1.5
Clutch release bearing bracket to gearbox housing	11/1.5
Fluid reservoir to lower and upper brackets (Ferodo converter)	16/2
Lower cover plate to clutch housing (nut)	16/2
Lower cover plate to clutch housing (screw)	12/1.7
Upper cover plate to clutch housing	11/1.5
Link, push rod to clutch fork	5/0.7
Lower and upper fluid reservoir brackets to body (Ferodo converter)	16/2
Slave cylinder to clutch housing	16/2
Ball joint to control tube	5/0.7
Ball joint bracket to floor	5/0.7
Ball joint cage to selector lever	11/1.5
Ball joint rod adjustable box	16/2
Cable bracket to gearbox control cover	11/1.5
Cable sheath nut: (near gear box)	18/2.5
(near floor bracket)	32/4.5
Cable nut	7/1
Control housing to gearbox	9/1
Drain plug	25/3.5
Fork control lever to shaft	11/1.5
Gearshift control outer lever to inner lever	7/1
Gearshift lever assembly to floor	11/1.5
Gearbox housing to clutch and differential housing	16/2
Idler bearing to rack and pinion housing	11/1.5
Obturator plate to control housing	9/1
Oil filler plug	25/3.5
Rear cover to gearbox housing	9/1

Reverse gear fork to shaft	11/1.5
Selector lever to control tube	7/1
Bearings and rings to mainshaft locking	108/15
Third and fourth gear fork to shaft	11/1.5
First and second gear fork to shaft	11/1.5
Differential crown wheel to differential box	40/5.5
Differential retaining plate to housing	16/2
Drain plug	25/3.5
Differential-clutch housing to cylinder block	33/4.5
Filler plug	25/3.5
Gearbox cover to housing	16/2

Front Suspension

Ft. Lbs./ Kgm.

Adjusting nut on link	
Adjusting lever to crossmember	54/7.5
Bracket, stabilizer bar to side member	16/2
Bearing to front wheel spindle	144/20
Crossmember to side member	36/5
Disc to wheel hub	36/5
Disc brake caliper to front wheel spindle	36/5
Lower ball joint to front wheel spindle	253/35
Lower ball joint to arm	54/7.5
Lower crossmember to body	36/5
Metal-rubber insulator to upper arm bolt	40/5.5
Metal-rubber insulator to lower arm bolt	54/7.5
Rubber bumper to lower arm	16/2
Road wheel shaft to hub	144/20
Steering stop to arm	16/2
Shock absorber upper end	9/1
Shock absorber lower end	16/2
Shock absorber lower bracket to arm	54/7.5
Stabilizer bar to link	16/2
Upper ball joint to front wheel spindle	25/3.5
Upper arm bracket to body	36/5
Upper crossmember to arm bracket	16/2
Upper arm to bracket	36/5

Rear Suspension

Ft. Lbs./ Kgm.

Adjusting lever to anchor bracket	54/7.5
Adjusting nut to link	
Adjusting lever to joint tube	5/0.7
Brake plate to arm	16/2
Drum to hub	9/1
Hinge bracket to outer bracket	47/6.5
Hinge bracket to inner bracket	51/7
Inner attachment of rear crossmember to body	83/11.5
Link to stabilizer bar	16/2
Link to arm	16/2
Outer attachment of rear crossmember to body	83/11.5
Rear wheel spindle	11/1.5
Shock absorber lower end to wheel spindle	16/2
Shock absorber upper end	9/1
Stabilizer bar brasket to anchor bracket	12/1.7
Screw locking under head	5/0.7

Steering

Ft. Lbs./ Kgm.

Ball joint to steering arm	22/3
Joint bracket to steering rack	54/7.5
Lock nut of pusher adjusting nut	43/6

Rack pinion and flexible joint to steering shaft	7/1
Steering rack bracket to side member	16/2
Steering rack to bracket	16/2
Steering rack pinion	40/5.5
Steering link to joint	36/5
Steering wheel to steering shaft	40/5.5
Universal joint yoke to upper part of steering shaft	7/1

Brakes

Brake master cylinder to pedal bracket	7/1
Handbrake to car body	16/2
Handbrake rod to equalizer	7/1
Pedal bracket assembly to cowl panel	7/1
Pedal bracket assembly upper part to cowl panel	22/3
Sheath retainer to front crossmember	16/2

Tightening Specifications

Simca 1000

Engine Head and Block

Ft. Lbs./ Kgm.

Cylinder head to block screws	45/6.2
Intake manifold nuts	12/1.6
Exhaust manifold nuts	16/2.2
Rocker arm screws and nuts	12/1.6
Rocker arm shaft screws	7/1
Spark plugs	20/2.8
Water temperature thermocontact to engine (1000 Coupe)	18/2.5
Water temperature thermocontact	11/1.5
Water outlet elbow and cap screws	7/1
Gear box screws and nuts	35/4.7
Oil pressure switch	25/3.5
Oil pressure feeler connector to engine (1000 Coupe)	20/2.7
Oil pressure feeler to connector (1000 Coupe)	15/2
Block drain plug	15/2
Oil pan screws	7/1
Timing gear cover screws and nuts	7/1
Stay bracket screws and nuts	7/1
Fuel pump mounting screws	15/2
Starter mounting screws	15/2
Generator to block mounting screws	34/4.7
Generator adjust arm to bracket screw	15/2
Timing gear to camshaft screw	7/1
Oil pump cover screws	7/1
Oil pump relief valve plug	23/3.2
Oil strainer to timing gear cover screw and nut	15/2
Oil strainer to bracket screw	7/1
Flywheel cover plate screws	16/2.2
Carburetor mounting nuts	15/2

Engine Suspension

Ft. Lbs./ Kgm.

Supporting leaf to bracket screw	17/2.4
Leaf and bracket to rear crossmember	17/2.4

Leaf stop and bracket to rear suspension crossmember	17/2.4
Suspension yoke to gearbox rear cover screws	52/7.2
Leaf to engine front suspension yoke nut	38/5.2
Engine support to cylinder block screws	16/2.2
Engine support crossmember to body nuts and screws	34/4.7
Engine upper support shaft nuts	9/1.2
Suspension stay to engine and to crossmember nuts	15/2

Crankshaft and Connecting Rods

Ft. Lbs./Kgm.

Flywheel to crankshaft screws	22/3
Crankshaft main bearing cap screws	47/6.5
Crankshaft rear bearing sealing shell screws	7/1
Connecting rod cap screws	17/2.3
Oil centrifugal separator center screw	58/8
Oil centrifugal separator cover screws	7/1

Water Pump and Fan

Ft. Lbs./Kgm.

Water pump mounting nuts	13/1.9
Water pump supporting arm screws and nuts	15/2
Water pump cover screws and nuts	15/2
Pulley to water pump shaft nut	41/5.7
Fan pulley nuts (from engine No. 5017146)	29/4

Exhaust System

Ft. Lbs./Kgm.

Exhaust pipe to muffler	8.7/1.2
Muffler to front and rear brackets	16/2.2
Muffler front bracket to engine	16/2.2
Collar to exhaust pipe and exhaust manifold	16/2.2

Clutch

Ft. Lbs./Kgm.

Fork shaft to clutch housing nuts	6/.8
Flywheel cover plate and exhaust muffler front bracket screws	16/2.2
Clutch housing to gearbox screws	34/4.7
Clutch to flywheel screws	7/1
Clutch cylinder to clutch housing screws	16/2.2

Transaxle

Ft. Lbs./Kgm.

Ring gear to rear axle carrier screws	47/6.5
Rear axle sealing cap to support screws	15/2
Rear axle bearing caps screws	34/4.7
Bearing retaining plates to secondary shaft screws	16/2.2
Bearing to secondary shaft retaining nut	130/18
Front cover to transaxle housing screws	16/2.2
Forks and shift to shaft screws	7/1
Control cover to transaxle housing screws	16/2.2

Control tube bearing support to floor panel screws	7/1
Tie rod to control tube and shift shaft to transaxle housing screws and nuts	16/2.2
Wheel shaft and flexible coupling locking nut	123/17
Half wheel shaft to flexible coupling screws	34/4.7

Front Suspension

Ft. Lbs./Kgm.

Reinforcing plate to frame screws	16/2.2
Bracket and leaf spring reinforcing plate screws	34/4.7
Lower ball joint and shock absorber bracket to leaf spring screw	15/2
Lower arm to bushing locking nuts	40/5.5
Upper arm to frame nuts	34/4.7
Ball joints to front wheel spindle nuts	45/6.2
Shock absorber lower end screws and nuts	34/4.7
Shock absorber upper end nuts	9/1.2
Rubber bumper to frame nut	7/1

Rear Suspension

Ft. Lbs./Kgm.

Crossmember to frame screws	34/4.7
Suspension arm shaft to bushing locking and screws and nuts	34/4.7
Suspension arm to crossmember screws and nuts	34/4.7
Shock absorber upper and lower end nuts	9/1.2
Shock absorber support to suspension arm screws	16/2.2

Steering

Ft. Lbs./Kgm.

Steering gear housing screws	16/2.2
Housing to floor panel nuts	7/1
Steering idler arm screws	16/2.2
Ball joint locking nuts	22/3
Steering stabilizer nuts	16/2.2
Steering shaft to steering gear housing screw	16/2.2
Steering wheel nut	38/5.2

Brakes

Ft. Lbs./Kgm.

Front and rear plate screws and nuts	34/4.7
Front and rear brake drum screws	7/1
Front and rear cylinder to plate screws	6.5/0.9
Brake line to connectors	15/2
Four-way connector to floor panel screw	12/1.7
Handbrake rear cable to frame screw	45/6.2
Disc brake caliper to bracket screws and nuts (1000 Coupe)	33/4.5
Disc brake assemblies to front wheel spindles and suspension arm screws and nuts (1000 Coupe)	34/4.7